Architectural Development in the Earliest Settled Agricultural Phases of Azerbaijan

Mubariz S. Azimov

BAR International Series 1467
2006

Published in 2016 by
BAR Publishing, Oxford

BAR International Series 1467

Architectural Development in the Earliest Settled Agricultural Phases of Azerbaijan

ISBN 978 1 84171 903 0

© M S Azimov and the Publisher 2006

The author's moral rights under the 1988 UK Copyright,
Designs and Patents Act are hereby expressly asserted.

All rights reserved. No part of this work may be copied, reproduced, stored,
sold, distributed, scanned, saved in any form of digital format or transmitted
in any form digitally, without the written permission of the Publisher.

BAR Publishing is the trading name of British Archaeological Reports (Oxford) Ltd.
British Archaeological Reports was first incorporated in 1974 to publish the BAR
Series, International and British. In 1992 Hadrian Books Ltd became part of the BAR
group. This volume was originally published by Archaeopress in conjunction with
British Archaeological Reports (Oxford) Ltd / Hadrian Books Ltd, the Series principal
publisher, in 2006. This present volume is published by BAR Publishing, 2016.

Printed in England

BAR titles are available from:

              BAR Publishing
              122 Banbury Rd, Oxford, OX2 7BP, UK
EMAIL   info@barpublishing.com
PHONE +44 (0)1865 310431
FAX   +44 (0)1865 316916
              www.barpublishing.com

Contents

Prologue	iii
Foreword	v
List of Illustrations	vii
Introduction	1
The General Characteristics of the Cultural Monuments Investigated	5
The Processes of Cultural Development and the Construction Layers	7
The Structure of Settlement Planning	11
The Constructions and their Architecture	19
Decision-making and the constructions; reconstructions	24
The functions of constructions	35
Conclusions	39
Bibliography	41
Illustrations	47

Prologue

This short study is the fruit of much field, archival and laboratory research. The background to the book was laborious, but the pleasure of realizing my dream to present before the scientific community the cultural heritage of Azerbaijan far outweighs any difficulties. You are all invited to visit the unique monuments of Azerbaijan for yourselves and share my feelings.

For me this work was invaluable - it has become part of my life - but its merit is for others to judge. I would be happy to receive readers' comments directly at the address below.

Mubariz S. Azimov
E-mail: mubariz_az@mail.ru, mubariz_az@hotmail.com

Foreword

Scientific research on those cultural monuments representing the earliest agricultural settlement and domestication phases of Azerbaijan began with the excavations at Kultepe 1 in 1951. The last 50 years have seen the investigation of many monuments in all areas of Azerbaijan. The findings of these researches have been included in many scientific works.

Analysis of the scientific literature demonstrates a high level of archaeological study in the culture of the earliest agro-pastoral period of Azerbaijan. However, in all this literature the architecture of the investigated culture has not been presented in any depth. Architectural information and the recorded data reveal the descriptive characteristics of monuments, and especially historical directivity.

Research on most ancient monuments tends to break down during cultural hiatuses, awaiting clarification by the analysis of those architects who specialize in archaeological excavations. The archaeological record for Azerbaijan, and not only Azerbaijan, includes archaeological excavations not undertaken by expert architects. The majority of archaeologists were not interested in building remains as, at first sight, they appeared to be of little scientific value. The result was that whole settlements disappeared, without appropriate records, at the cost of invaluable and irreplaceable information regarding site architecture.

A similar situation applies regarding the scientific study of architectural culture, and obliges us to investigate subject and technique based on a few specific examples: in our case the study of ancient architectural remains by means of archaeological excavation. Taking into account the complexity of the subject and its geographical and chronological extents, we have concentrated on certain questions of wider interest:

- The appearance of man and his distribution in Azerbaijan with regard to the process of transformation of temporary settlements into settlement phases.
- The mechanics of the formation of cultural and construction layers.
- The structures of settlement planning.
- The form, design, and functional features of constructions.
- The genetic development of the architecture of Azerbaijan.

The development of these questions has required research into a huge quantity of diverse sources, particularly archives. It is important to note at this point that some material was unavailable, even from within certain archives. In some reports of archaeological expeditions there were no figures or graphic drawings which are so necessary for our research.

Special attention has been paid to primary sources, such as the reports of archaeological expeditions, field notes, and the first-hand measurements of monuments. For fuller explanations of some questions, personal meetings with archaeologists were held, including I.H. Narimanov, G.S. Ismailov, J.N. Rustamov, F.M. Muradova, V.H. Aliev, and G.M. Aslanov.

With regard to our researches into settlement planning, and where exact stratigraphical data was required, the valuable material accommodated within the Institute of the History of Academic Sciences of Azerbaijan was consulted. This included the reports of various archaeological expeditions between 1956-1999, and particularly investigations into the monuments of Kultepe-1, Toyretepe, Shomutepe, Gargalartepesi, Saritepe, Baba-Dervish, Ilanlitepe, Leylatepesi, Garakepektepe, Alikemektepesi, Chalagantepe and others.

This book investigates for the first time the complex processes involved with the occurrence and development of Eneolithic and Bronze Age architecture over the extent of Azerbaijan. The study also investigates the important questions left unanswered in the architectural, archaeological and ethnographic literature. For the first time, we were able to develop a planning structure for settlements, inhabited complexes, and units.

The fundamentals of the research have been stated in a number of publications, and have been reported at scientific conferences and sessions; they have been well received in scientific circles.

List of Illustrations

Fig. 1.	*The author*	47
Fig. 2.	*The author on site in Gobustan*	48
Fig. 3.	*Distribution map of monuments studied*	48
Fig. 4.	*Chalagantepe. General view of southern section of the excavation site*	49
Fig. 5.	*Chalagantepe. General view of northern section of the excavation site*	49
Fig. 6.	*Chalagantepe. Plan of level 405-390 cm*	50
Fig. 7.	*Chalagantepe. Plan of level 390-370 cm*	50
Fig. 8.	*Chalagantepe. Plan of level 370-350 cm*	51
Fig. 9.	*Chalagantepe. Plan of level 350-325 cm*	51
Fig. 10.	*Chalagantepe. Plan of level 325-305 cm*	52
Fig. 11.	*Chalagantepe. Plan of level 305-290 cm*	52
Fig. 12.	*Chalagantepe. Plan of level 290-275 cm*	53
Fig. 13.	*Chalagantepe. Plan of level 275-255 cm*	53
Fig. 14.	*Chalagantepe. Plan of level 255-230 cm*	54
Fig. 15.	*Chalagantepe. Plan of level 230-208 cm*	54
Fig. 16.	*Chalagantepe. Plan of level 208-190 cm*	55
Fig. 17.	*Chalagantepe. Plan of level above 190 cm*	55
Fig. 18.	*Chalagantepe. Consolidated plan of all levels (cut on an axis 1-1)*	56
Fig. 19.	*Chalagantepe. Pit-house dwelling 71*	56
Fig. 20.	*Chalagantepe. Reconstruction of level 255-230 cm*	57
Fig. 21.	*Chalagantepe. Reconstruction of level 290-275 cm*	58
Fig. 22.	*Chalagantepe. Building 26*	59
Fig. 23.	*Chalagantepe. Building 26*	59
Fig. 24.	*Chalagantepe. "Plano-convex brick" in wall masonry*	60
Fig. 25.	*Chalagantepe. Building 26. Plan of three levels of dwellings, cut and reconstruction*	60
Fig. 26.	*Chalagantepe. Furnace 31*	61
Fig. 27.	*Alikemektepesi. Plan of construction layer at level 480-380 cm*	62
Fig. 28.	*Alikemektepesi. Plan of construction layer at level 380-280 cm*	63
Fig. 29.	*Alikemektepesi. Plan of construction layer at level 310-210 cm*	64
Fig. 30.	*Alikemektepesi. Plan of construction layer at level 215-130 cm*	65
Fig. 31.	*Alikemektepesi. Reconstruction of settlement at level 310-210 cm*	66
Fig. 32.	*Toyretepe. Plans and cut 1-1*	67
Fig. 33.	*Toyretepe. Reconstruction of level 430-340 cm*	68
Fig. 34.	*Toyretepe. Reconstruction of level 290-240 cm*	68
Fig. 35.	*Leylatepesi. Plan of excavation site*	69
Fig. 36.	*Shomutepe. Plan and cut of excavation site*	70
Fig. 37.	*Shomutepe. Reconstruction*	70
Fig. 38.	*Gargalartepesi. Plan of level 410-340 cm*	71
Fig. 39.	*Gargalartepesi. Plan of level 360-300 cm*	71
Fig. 40.	*Gargalartepesi. Reconstruction of level 360-300 cm.*	72
Fig. 41.	*Gargalartepesi. Plan of level 300-270 cm*	72
Fig. 42.	*Gargalartepesi. Plan of level 270-245 cm*	73
Fig. 43.	*Gargalartepesi. Consolidated plan of all layers*	73
Fig. 44.	*Ilanlitepe. Plan of excavation site*	74
Fig. 45.	*Ilanlitepe. Reconstruction*	74
Fig. 46.	*Kultepe 1. Plan, cut and reconstruction. Early Bronze Age V layer. Level 11.35 m*	75
Fig. 47.	*Baba-Dervish. Hill II. Plan, cut and reconstruction.*	76
Fig. 48.	*Guneshtepe. Plan, cut and reconstruction of Early Bronze Age layer.*	76
Fig. 49.	*Garakepektepe. Early Bronze Age layer. Plan, cut and reconstruction.*	77

Introduction

Archaeological research over recent decades has allowed more precise dating for the settlement of Azerbaijan. The earliest settlement of man in Azerbaijan occurred in Lower Palaeolithic times. Amongst the oldest of Palaeolithic monuments is the cave at Azikh, with its deepest level finds from the Lower Palaeolithic. Man has been active in Azerbaijan for 1.2 million years (27, p.71).

The subsequent Palaeolithic and Mesolithic periods are represented by many interesting finds in caves and open-air settlements. Mesolithic settlements (10th-9th millennium BC), such as those distinguished in the lowest levels at Keniza, Firuz, Ana Zaga (43, pp.504-505), the Mesolithic level of the Dashsalahli cave, the settlement at Garakepektepe (30, p.6) etc., were not seasonal. They were long-term settlements and have preserved significant cultural layers.

Over the following historical phases appear the first settlements of the earliest agro-pastoral period. The oldest of them, using radiocarbon dating, is Shomutepe (5560 +/- 70 BC, JIE-631). The dates of the majority of similar settlements are set within the framework of the 5th millennium BC. To the final Eneolithic stage belong the settlements of Baba-Dervish (Lowest), Leylatepesi, Alikemektepesi, and Ilanlitepe - dated to the end of the 5th to the early 4th millennium BC.

The early Kur-Araz Culture is dated to the second half of the 4th millennium BC. This implies that the Kur-Araz later phases are to be taken as the middle, or initial centuries of the second half of the 3rd millennium BC (30, p.31).

The new extensive settlements were formed by the development of the early agro-pastoral period, concurrent with the expansion of existing settlements. Significant construction was required to satisfy the needs of the growing population, and this promoted the development of original architecture and the appropriate construction technology.

In deepest antiquity, the nature and climate of Azerbaijan provided a favourable environment for man and for the development of a subsistence economy. These favourable climatic conditions encouraged in Azerbaijan such settlements as Lower Palaeolithic Azikh. The climate of the region has repeatedly changed over time, but the environment has always supported man, as is demonstrated by the significant cultural layers found in the cave at Azikh (26, p.3-12).

In the Kur-Araz period, the lowland areas, for the most part, were suitable for agriculture. The same was true of the valleys of the river Araz, the Iranian plateau, and the Lenkeran lowland. Cattle breeding developed, thanks to the grasses that covered the mountains above the valleys, even in the dry summer months.

Thus the ecological conditions and climate of Azerbaijan were perfectly suited to the type of environment necessary for the transition from a hunter-gathering to an early farming economy. In turn, the new economic system fuelled the rapid development of construction and an architectural complex.

The most ancient settlements of Azerbaijan are those monuments located on the plains and wide river valleys. They were located typically by smaller rivers and other water sources which, over time, became less abundant, often drying up entirely. This situation explains the resettlement patterns of the Early Bronze Age. The changes in the ecological environment forced the peoples of the Kur-Araz Culture to leave areas along the river Kur, Garabag, Mil and Mugan Steppes — previously populated by the earliest farmers and settlers — and to relocate to more mountainous regions where the rivers were still deep enough to support their activities. Hence, in explaining the settlement movements of the Eneolithic Period and Kur-Araz Culture in Azerbaijan, different factors apply, but the key distinctions arise not as a result of any change to the principle of moving, but rather to changes in the ecological environment. Resettlement due to climactic conditions is a well-understood phenomenon of the Eneolithic -Early Bronze Age.

The main groups of the earliest settlements are located in the areas of Lake Urmia, in Nakhchivan, in Mugan, Mil, the Garabag Steppes, the Ganja-Gazakh region, and in Gobustan (*Fig.3*).

The rich and varied natural conditions of Southern Azerbaijan promoted the occurrence here of the first farming settlements — Geytepe, Hasanlu, Haji Firuz, Dalmatepe, Pijdelitepe, Yaniktepe, etc. The majority of these are concentrated in the areas of Lake Urmia and along the banks of the rivers flowing into it (14, p.138), and are typically represented by artificial mounds, often revealing breaks in continuity over different periods.

The main flow of the River Araz enters the Sederek plain, where the spurs of the Daralagez Mountains are separated from the brackish plain of Beyukduz. The current of the River Nakhchivanchay separates it from the Nakhchivan plain. Northwest, the Agri plain stretches away from the River Araz. Agriculture in this zone is only possible by irrigation, and this has resulted in some soil contamination by salts. For this reason the settlements here are located in separate groups. In one of those, in a valley of the Nakhchivanchay River, are the settlements of Kultepe 1 and Kultepe 2, with significant cultural remains of the Eneolithic and Bronze Ages. Apart from these two sites, AEneolithic material is restricted to settlements near the villages of Shahtakhti and Sederek.

The earliest Eastern peripatetic tribes are traceable up to the Caspian Sea, as the monuments at Gobustan and Mugan testify (39, p.88). The Mugan settlements have developed on the raised, southern part of the Steppe, along the banks of the smaller rivers. One group of settlements is on the eastern fringe of the city of Jalilabad. This, the Misharchay 2-6 Settlement, has exclusively Eneolithic finds. Another group of settlements is located along the dry and small Quru-Dere channel. The settlement of Alikemektepesi, with cultural levels dating to the Eneolithic and Early Bronze Age, fringes the village of Uchtepe, on a high terrace along the right bank of the Injechay River.

In Gobustan, most of the ancient monuments show traces of change. Other early settlements, showing insignificant Eneolithic traces, are firmly linked to the rocky mountains of Beyukdash, Kichikdash, and Jingirdag. The Early Bronze Age settlement that was found on the open space below Mt. Beyukdash was also dependent on local water sources. It was part of a circuit of numerous and fine settlements located on rocky outcrops below mountains.

In Mil and Garabag on the Steppe, the oldest settlements are divided into western and eastern groups. In the western, higher part, settlements of different size have now been investigated. In the eastern Steppe part, Eneolithic settlement levels are insignificant, having been overlayed by later periods. The reason for this, probably, was a gradual reduction in the rivers which would dry up in periods of drought. The important Eneolithic settlements (Shomulutepe, Kultepe, Rasultepe, Ilanlitepe, Chalagantepe, Leylatepesi, etc.) are concentrated into large groups, 15-25 km from the mountains. A number of settlements are located on the lower reaches of the River Khachinchay. A large group of settlements is located on the banks of the now dry plain of the Agri channel of the Khachinchay River, heading southeast from the settlement of Bash Gervend. Some of the settlements on Garabag Steppe are located along ravines that were formed from the outflow of underground water. The settlements located in the now waterless places include it, Chalagantepe, Gonshutepe and Gabirsanligtepe, of which there are no later cultural remains. Near these settlements, quite probably in the Eneolithic era, there would have passed a channel of the Gargarchay River, which flows for 5-6 km. Eneolithic settlements on the right bank of the River Gargarchay have not been firmly located. This is explained, apparently, by the significant height and steepness of the right-hand bank. To date, more than 40 settlements have been investigated on the Garabag plain.

A similar situation occurs at Mil Steppe. Two settlement groups (representing about 10 settlements) have been investigated here, both directly linked to nearby water sources.

More than 20 settlements on the main channel of the River Kur are found on the Ganja-Gazakh plain, especially near the Rivers Aqstafachay and Gasansu. These have deep beds and flow through the plain between the Small Caucasus and the River Kur. There are no other significant rivers in this zone. The River Gasansu, running from the mountain gorge onto the plain (near the Eneolithic settlement of Shomutepe), probably formed channels of various sizes. One channel has been traced flowing parallel to the river, and the presence of this channel, and others like it, explain the development of the settlements of Shomutepe, Toyretepe, Jinnitepe, Arzamastepesi, etc. When water volumes in these channels reduced and began to dry up, the Eneolithic populations dependent on them abandoned the settlements. Life on these hillsides resumed much later, towards the end of the Bronze Age.

Other settlement groups, all linked to the Shomutepe Culture, were arranged on the main stream of the Kur River (to the right of Khramchay). The earliest settlements here are found on the plain, on the banks, or near the rivers. These settlements are all at a certain distance from the mountains, and share a topographical identity. The exception is the small settlement of Sioni, with its remains of stone buildings. It is located in a mountain gorge to the west of the Kvemo-Kartli plain. This settlement obviously developed later than all the other known settlements on this plain.

Ancient 'tell' settlements have not yet been found to the north of the River Kur. The rare and rather scanty remains show a totally different settlement structure, the reasons for which are unknown. The presence of similar settlements far to the northeast (in the territory of Dagestan) shows that the early population reached these areas (25, p.104).

With regard to the map of settlement distribution, it is possible to ascertain that all the local settlement groups are in dry, continental-strip zones, where traditionally the cultivation of cereals was practised. At the same time, these zones were covered with the plentiful grass required for cattle breeding. It is relevant to investigate the geographical and climatic conditions in play when trying to find the primary reasons for similar distribution patterns of ancient settlements.

The General Characteristics of the Cultural Monuments Investigated.

The settlements of the earliest agro-pastoral phase were founded, usually, on hill mounds. As a rule they are based on alluvial ground, having an even horizontal plane with a differing vegetative covering, and therefore stand clearly in the surrounding natural landscape. Settlement heights show a large variety — from low to high, and over small or large areas. It is necessary to note that ploughing activity over time has altered the contours of some of the mounds. The ground levels around the mounds have risen by, on average, 1 m, and this has had the effect of reducing the heights of mound settlements in relation to modern day surface levels.

Taking the above into account, it may be assumed that the mounds appeared higher during the time periods under discussion. Thus, the greatest size of these mounds will relate to the discontinuance of life on them. Dating and stratigraphy of these settlements may show that, in the 6th millennium BC, when they were first put to agricultural use and domestication, the inhabitants settled directly on level ground. In the 5th millennium BC some increase in settlements may already be traced, for example at Shomutepe, Toyretepe, Gargalartepesi, Chalagantepe, Haji Firuz, Hajilar, etc. The greatest heights were already reached by the 4th-3rd millennium BC, as a result of the accumulation of layers from the Early Bronze Age (the Kur-Araz Culture).

The most significant Eneolithic layer at Kehriztepe is at 10-12 m, and at Gargalartepesi at about 10m (36, p.83). At Kultepe 1 it is reached at 9.4m (22, 4-13m) (18, p.24), at Toyretepe at 5.5m, at Alikemektepesi at 5.1m, at Khantepe at 5m (1, p.76), at Chalagantepe at 4.4m, at Shomutepe at 2.5 m, and at Ilanlitepe at 1.5m (36, p.17, 57).

The Early Bronze Age period layers at Kultepe 1 are at about 9.5m (18, p.80), at Garakepektepe at more than 7m (30, p.6) and on Baba-Dervish 1 up to 1m (29, p.11). The above makes clear that there is a wide variance in the separation of the cultures, indicated by the different durations of accumulations.

On a horizontal plane, the settlements are round or oval in form: rectangular or oblong settlements are thus far unknown. This is explained by settlements developing around a united core formed in earlier times, when all settlements concentrated around a common courtyard and made a functionally united system.

The settlement areas themselves were usually small — about 0.5 hectares, although very small and very large settlements do exist, such as at Khinitepe (c. 5 hectares), Polutepe (c. 4 hectares), and Gargalartepesi (c. 2 hectares).

It does not follow, however, that all areas of the settlement were occupied simultaneously. Researches show that sometimes a large part of any settlement area might have remained unpopulated. The reasons for this phenomenon will be considered below.

Also deserving attention, are the characteristic defensive walls of some of the larger settlements: Kultepe 2, Oglangala, Chalkhangala, Vaykhir Gavurgala, Gazanchigala, Garakepektepe, Daire, and Kelbejer.

In the upper levels of the Early Bronze layer at Garakepektepe there are some excavated remains (about 20 m) of a defensive wall made from stone fragments (30, p.7). It is reasonable to assume that there were similar walls strengthening the characteristic settlements of Meynetepe, Shomulutepe, Kultepe, etc.

In Gobustan, the small Bronze Age settlement at Daire (3rd millennium BC) was investigated (6, 21, p.79), and the settlement layout was defined by a round defensive wall, 48 m. in diameter. The wall is impressive — up to 1 m in width, and made from selected fieldstones.

A similar Early Bronze settlement has been found in the high mountains of Kelbejer (30, p.7). It is located on a high, flat plateau, protected on three sides by deep gorges. The remains of a well-defended round structure have been uncovered, surrounded by walls 22 m in diameter and 2 m wide. These walls were constructed of river boulders and volcanic stone. The internal area here (as with Daire), is divided into numerous spaces.

There is a similar defensive system at Bronze Age Kultepe 2, including a formidable wall 2 m wide (22, pp.17-20). It is built of large river boulders, huge stones, and crude bricks.

The Processes of Cultural Development and the Construction Layers

The formation of hill settlements is the result of a long-term and complex process. The majority of settlements arise at a location that was once a stopping point (with insignificant cultural remains) or a similar modest site. The first constructions on many of them were erected on unprepared ground. Over time the settlement gradually rose as a result of such factors as dwelling and building activity, the compression of old buildings, infilling, constructions for non-domestic activity, the disposal of rubbish and ashes, etc. It is worth noting that, at the start of the settlement, clay for construction was extracted partially from the immediate area and that this activity had a bearing on the layer accumulation process. Furthermore, when a settlement's total area had been developed, the building clay had to be 'imported' from outside the settlement area and this further encouraged expansion of cultural activity and remains. Intensive settlement growth was promoted by an original economy of colonisers and, within any settlement, everything had to be brought in to the community and almost nothing was removed. If to all this was added what was buried by earlier generations, then the reasons for the intensive growth in cultural deposits become obvious.

In researching such intensive growth in any cultural layer, an understanding of the nature of the building materials, and the relative instability of the constructions, is important. Evidence comes from the building remains themselves, where the crude bricks and clay mass could not be reused as basic material. At the destruction of older buildings, all the material was used for footings and foundations, for infilling separate areas within a courtyard, etc. A secondary observation is that construction took place on a frequent basis. By our accounts, most of the durable construction required attention, or renovation, about every five years (not to mention annual running repairs). It is interesting to note that in mountain areas, with identical conditions and with the same building materials available, no mound settlements have been found. Where mound settlements arose, the colonisers benefited from the additional protection afforded against flooding, as well as improved drainage, sanitation, and collection of rain water, etc.

Excavations on these mounds show that the accumulation of cultural layers on different sites was not necessarily the same, especially where there was intensive filling or covering with dust, ashes and debris. This is noticeable on level 1-1 at Chalagantepe (*Fig.18*), where a foundation structure intrudes above an inhabited level at 50-60 cm.

Debates still arise over the intensity of the substantial deposits of cultural remains. This question has never been the subject of special research, and, consequently, some serious mistakes have developed, in particular with regard to the interpretation of the apparent overlaying of several construction layers in one construction block. When this occurs, the planning outlines of the construction projects appear to block each other. Some suggest that particular construction layers contain evidence of different periods of reorganisation (34, p.30). Other authors are inclined to believe that one building layer cannot intrude into the following one (2, pp.53-70). If this is the case, some construction layers may encompass a thick mass of up to 2 metres. To compound matters further, there has even been a recent practice of linking the results of a particular archaeological season to a distinct construction layer. The scale of the problem in this area is self-evident.

Things become a little clearer if we consider one or two accounts. At the settlements of Chalagantepe, Gargalartepesi, and Shulaveris-Gora, constructions to a residual height of

2m have been exposed. This suggests that the walls of these constructions existed when the formation of the two-metre cultural break finally blocked their remains. Javakhishvili A.I. writes that these constructions have existed for 700 years. We should note immediately that in relation to the accounts of these constructions, as far as we have them, they could have existed for no more than 20-30 years. O.H. Habibullaev makes a reasonable argument based on careful analysis for his case that certain constructions (with wall thicknesses of 30-40 cm) lasted for 35-40 years within the Eneolithic layer at Kultepe 1 (18, p.189). If taking into account the numerous reorganisations of the different layers that represent continuous utilization of the same construction, it is feasible that the most long-lived constructions might have lasted for 150 years or so. In this case, it is obvious that a break in a cultural layer that overlaps the remains of a construction should represent the same interval of time. On this basis, the formation of a 2-metre cultural level suggests a maximum time span of 150 years.

Our experience of archaeological excavation, and the study of the formation processes of cultural layers, show that the accumulation of cultural breaks happened continuously (19, p.46; 20, pp.80-81). This is precisely demonstrated at a section of Chalagantepe (*Fig. 18*). These sections were prepared by us from the walls of the excavation and represent a standard for the study of the character of cultural breaks at similar monuments. As is visible from these sections, there is no natural stratification of cultural layers at this settlement site. The layers traced on a section do not overlap the edges of the one or two constructions there. This seems to hold for all the sites excavated, and is not out of the ordinary. At a continuously occupied site, such as Chalagantepe, these layers are not formed. The cultural layer develops gradually here into a thick mass. The outline of the layers is a result of intensive construction activity and spasmodic architectonic changes on sites of limited area. These restricted sites enforce techniques of vertical planning, such as levelling, building varied platforms, and works of construction and reconstruction. The limiting of the layered area in a section testifies to the partial, instead of general, re-planning of a site.

The question about degrees of total reorganisation is disputable and, so far, not developed in the special literature. Providing an answer here, however, would allow us at once to reach some important objectives such as defining structural planning, studying the technology of construction manufacture, and exploring the general concepts of settlement development. These are all highly important areas as they help explain the formation processes of any cultural layer. It is necessary to point out that, despite the importance of the question, its discussion has to bring in aspects of surfaces and discrepancies, which has resulted in many publications reaching tendentious conclusions concerning the "general re-planning of large sites". Some authors acknowledge similar re-planning, but only in terms of the overall settlement which should be obvious without special research. It is clear that a whole settlement territory could not be made habitable simultaneously.

At the Alikemektepesi settlement there is a layer 20-30 cm thick (2, p.58) between the wall remains of the 3rd construction layer, and between the floor remains of the buildings of the 2nd construction layer. This area was used at some time as a burial place, and for non-domestic purposes - pottery, etc. Some tombs, as well as remains of furnace glazing, have been found here, and they have been overlain by dwellings. This demonstrates that the area was not abandoned for long, and that normal life carried on at other locations within the settlement. Reasons for this temporary abandonment could be explained by the demands of other complex building and free sites elsewhere (*Figs. 29, 30*).

At Shomutepe, a pit, 10 x 2 x 2 m, was opened near the settlement, probably for clay production for building (35, p.46) (*Fig. 35*). Later, it was filled with ashes, refuse, etc., and constructions were erected over it. Hence, external locations were gradually opened, filled, and then built upon. In this way the site of Shomutepe expanded over time and was not developed simultaneously.

A pit 6.5 m wide and 1.25 m deep has been revealed at Imiris-Gora (28, p.40). The excavator has not explained this feature, but it is our opinion that, as at Shomutepe, this pit was dug for a similar non-domestic purpose.

These above two examples further illustrate that settlement development is a complex, multilateral process, as much progression as regression, the whole of which characterizes the dynamics of the community and its constructions. That there was continuous occupation of the excavated site at Chalagantepe, one has only to investigate layer 270 cm (from level 180 cm up to topsoil at level 450 cm).

On the basis of the foregoing, it is possible to establish that the cultural layers of a settlement were accumulated continuously, forming a uniform mass. The changes in tonal colouring of a layer, and its inclusions, depend on the change of character in the waste, and on the changes in function of separate sites. As to the traceable levels of any cultural layer (of whatever scale), they are formed as a result of intensive construction activity alternating with regressive phenomena.

At this point, it is necessary to consider the opinions of other experts that differ from ours. Concerning the reasons for the formation of a thick mass of cultural layers, some authors are inclined to consider that this was due to the quick exhaustion of space around a settlement, and that the population was compelled to occupy new space. Thus they moved to new settlements and returned at a later date. Fixed terms of 10 years for field exhaustion, and 50 years for regeneration are typically given (15, pp.169-170). Moreover, the thesis is put forward that long-term agricultural activity results, eventually, in such significant changes of living, even climatic, conditions that the population is compelled finally to leave (32, p.144).

On our site, the above statements, especially the latter, have no serious foundation if one remembers that for most ancient settlements the debate centres on the time of site formation. In AEneolithic times, the population was insignificant in relation to the huge areas of fertile land occupied, and the economic opportunities of the population were so limited that they could hardly cause structural changes to the field and soil, and least of all have an effect on climatic conditions.

Hence, it is to the actual mechanics of development that one should look for reasons why thick layers formed in a settlement. If there is no evidence of fire, or mass destruction of the population, other reasons for abandonment might include some form of pollution to the environment in and around the settlement, illness or epidemic, infestation of rodents, etc. In all these cases, former settlements could be occupied anew in due course, but new settlements, in these cases, will have little in common with the earlier ones, except for the generality of the site.

The above-stated and complex character of a cultural layer (expressed by the juxtaposition of construction remains among residual building materials and remnants of the local economy) presents significant difficulties in terms of any architectural study. The first stage is to understand the settlement planning and its component elements - inhabited units, inhabited complexes and groups — the dynamic development of which defines the structure of planning development.

To simplify this complex question we may divide a cultural layer into its constituent elements. An indivisible, homogeneous part of the cultural layer may impact on a certain horizontal surface plane, on which, at a concrete moment in time, inhabitation proceeded: such a plane can be fixed to a level of the cultural layer. The restoration of structures on this level will reflect a true picture of a settlement at that specific moment. A similar, inhabited level cannot accumulate a thick mass. That is, in three-dimensional measurement terms, to any possible values of X and Y, there corresponds only one constant meaning, Z (with a provision for any natural relief deflections). Hence, there is no room for error or choice. It is necessary only, during excavation, correctly to trace the inhabited level. Our experience has shown that this is quite possible.

Proceeding from this concrete model of what an inhabited level is, we may make certain generalisations with the aim of simplifying the study of settlement planning by allocating developmental planning phases within the limits of fixed time intervals covering the most significant changes. Obviously, the boundaries of the construction layers are artificial, but our generalisations are based on common criteria, in particular the definition of the top boundary. We have put in a common definition of scale for each construction layer by its three characteristic parameters:

1. First and foremost is the impossibility of the remains of one building to overlap another. It is obvious that previous buildings, and those constructed on their remains, could not coexist. They mutually exclude each other. There are short-term constructions that might overlap each other. These are destroyed in a short time and their building materials compressed into a platform, on which new buildings are constructed. Such short-term changes are easily differentiated within the cultural layer.

2. The second parameter for any construction layer is related to stratigraphic data. Data is required to fix the levels of the compressed courtyard platforms, building foundations, floor levels, etc. These measurements allow us, with absolute reliance, to define a chronological sequence of the construction of separate buildings.

3. The third important parameter for the construction layer is the architectural analysis of inhabited complexes and groups, making it easy to define the attitude of separate buildings to this or that construction layer.

Based on the above, 12 construction levels were selected from the cultural layer at Chalagantepe (2.7 m), covering from 15 cm to 30 cm of the layer. In this case the construction layer thickness was limited to 30 cm, otherwise the outlines of buildings would block each other. As to the actual identification of the construction layers, it had to be based on an artificial division within the guidelines of the generalisations adopted. Here we were guided by an optimality of variants, having fixed in each construction layer the most significant planning changes. Thereby, stratigraphically close constructions feature in each of the 12 construction layers: a dwelling group existing within a certain interval of time.

We have also applied our method to the construction layers and settlement planning at Shomutepe, Gargalartepesi, Toyretepe, Alikemektepesi, Leylatepesi, etc. (*Figs. 27-30, 32, 34, 37-40*).

The Structure of Settlement Planning

The above-mentioned treatment of the construction layers and their reconstructions, allow us to study settlement planning, track the movement, formation, and development of inhabited units, complexes, and groups, as well as to reveal the structured differences in their planning and why they might differ.

It is necessary to note that a study of settlement planning requires site excavation covering a minimum of two inhabited complexes that are functionally united organisms. They represent the core that will, finally, comprise the total settlement. Therefore, the archaeological record of even such a valuable monument as Kultepe 1 does not meet the necessary criterion, the excavation area studied being too restricted (*Fig. 44*). The excavation results have yielded valuable material relevant to the form of both Eneolithic and Bronze Age building design, but the limitation of the area studied has not provided sufficient information for analysis of settlement planning here. On the basis of similar material it is impossible to comment on the planning structure, it may be considered only in comparison with other similar monuments.

Similar situations apply to the settlements at Leylatepesi, Toyretepe, Baba-Dervish, Garakepektepe, Guneshtepe, etc., where the excavations undertaken did not reflect a complete picture of the settlement planning system employed (*Figs. 34, 32, 45, 47, 46*).

The basis of our work on planning study was provided by those settlements excavated over relatively larger areas, such as Alikemektepesi (396 sq. m.), Shomutepe (376 sq. m.), Chalagantepe (315 sq. m.), Gargalartepesi (216 sq. m.), and Ilanlitepe (216 sq. m.).

Analysis of settlement planning has revealed similarities in planning structure for the majority of cases. Overall planning seems to fall into two basic styles, determined by construction form.

The majority of settlements opted for round buildings, with an appropriate planning design. Examples are the sites at It, Kultepe 1, Kultepe 2, Baba-Dervish, Guneshtepe, Garakepektepe (lower level), Chalagantepe, Gargalartepesi, Shomutepe, Toyretepe, Yaniktepe, Alikemektepesi (3rd-5th levels), and Borispoltepe.

Settlements with rectangular buildings, with an appropriate planning design, are, Alikemektepesi (1st and 2nd levels), Leylatepesi, and Garakepektepe (upper level).

Exceptionally, Kultepe 1 has separate rectangular constructions with a set of rectangular extensions. Alikemektepesi (2nd level) is of oval construction. The Ilanlitepe settlement includes both forms of construction in the same layer.

The planning of the Ilanlitepe and Alikemektepesi settlements has some affinity. A feature of both settlements is that the planning includes separate constructions of a wide variety - from round and oval, to rectangular.

Ilanlitepe is peculiar in having no perfectly circular constructions, or exact wall cornering. The constructions here are either oval, semicircular, trapezoidal, or rectangular, all with rounded corners (*Fig. 42*). Three poorly defined, inhabited complexes (buildings 1, 7, 11) are indicated. Each complex consists of one basic and several areas for non-domestic functions. There are also contiguous and separate locations for non-domestic accommodation adjacent to the basic premises. Between these three complexes there are traces of two courtyards on an otherwise undeveloped site.

The Ilanlitepe settlement (4th millennium BC) could have had a large organization and a defined planning structure. This has been observed at other characteristic settlements such as Alikemektepesi, etc. At Alikemektepesi we managed to define the planning of 4 construction layers (Layers 1, 2, 3, and 4) at (1) 130-215 cm, (2) 210-310 cm, (3) 280-380 cm, (4) 380-480 cm (the repetition of some layers is explained by relief features - *Figs. 27-30*).

Of these, the 3rd and 4th layers were investigated over an area of 128 sq. m, and the 1st and 2nd layers over an area of 396 sq. m. The remains of two round constructions were found in the 4th layer, and the remains of five buildings and three intermediate walls were investigated in layer 3. From these remains, however, it is difficult to say much about the settlement planning as such. Clearly one construction had a basic circular plan (round-plan) and this form defined something of the plan. The subsequent two layers, excavated over an area of 396 sq. m, contained sufficient building remains to allow us to comment on their planning. The second construction layer is characterized basically by rectangular buildings. It is traced, typically, by a row of rectangular structures representing the main premises. They are grouped into four inhabited complexes. The two eastward ones, in an area otherwise free of constructions, are enclosed by walling. This lead to a development of inhabited complexes (with domestic and non-domestic premises) connected by a courtyard. Between these complexes there are free sites and passages. Taking into account the size of these complexes (the largest having seven premises, of which two were inhabited, it is feasible to assume that each belonged to one family. In the 1st layer, parts of the second structures were retained. The southern complex was also kept (with insignificant changes), but the three other complexes completely disappeared. On the site of the northern complex, there is a new inhabited complex (not completely defined). Determining the plan of this layer is complicated, as the western part of the excavation, and the area east of the southern complex, have had their subsequent construction works destroyed. The study of the construction layers at Alikemektepesi shows the originality of its planning structure which has no analogy in the Southern Caucasus or other regions. This originality is expressed in a plan that incorporates in its basic structure a system of separate inhabited units and courtyards that interact with other domestic and non-domestic buildings within the limits of a uniform complex.

The settlement at Garakepektepe is on the border of foothills and a lowland area, but its planning is characteristic of mountain settlements (*Fig. 47*). The settlement was built on the natural slope of a hill, and the construction, therefore, is graduated. The passages, streets, and platforms that remain between the buildings, as a rule, were covered with cobblestones or shingle (30, p.8).

The buildings investigated at Shomutepe allow us to group them in one construction layer (*Fig. 35*). Some of these constructions are located on the natural, others on a cultural layer that reaches under the VII construction up to 40 cm. Thus, the general mass of the layer reaches 40 cm. The settlement also has the remains of 20 buildings whose definite plans cannot now be traced. The selected sites are formed by walls that link the buildings. This is probably also characteristic of the planning structure. In the majority of buildings, the entrances remain and this allows us to plot their attitude to this or that complex. In the well-preserved central part three inhabited complexes have been traced, each of which consists of 2-3 buildings. The northern courtyard site is surrounded by five buildings and four intermediate walls. Of the five buildings, only three give on to the courtyard. In the two northern buildings, the entrances are inverted into the courtyard, i.e. they functionally relate to another complex.

The courtyard also had traces of a central rectangle dug into the natural and two pits close by. The central area is surrounded by six buildings, five with intermediate walls. Of the six buildings, only two relate to the complex — buildings III and 9 give on to the courtyard. In terms of its status as a complex, building IV is only at the first stage, and so does not afford much definition. In the second stage, when the intermediate wall between it and building III was orientated to the east, it could no longer be connected to the courtyard. Of the other three buildings, two belong to the northern complex and one to the southern. The courtyard of the central complex consists of two equal halves connected by a passage. Each of the two buildings leads into one of these halves. The southern complex is surrounded by five intermediate walls and three buildings, two of which give on to the courtyard.

All three complexes share the enclosed site of a courtyard, into which there is only one small access about 50 cm wide. In the northern complex, the entrance aperture is located on an intermediate wall that protects the courtyard from the northern part. In the central complex the entrance aperture is located in a wall laid between the III and IV buildings. In the southern complex, the access is via a corridor between the VI construction and an intermediate wall protecting the courtyard from the east. It is necessary to note that all three complexes have access to their different adjacent areas, but no access between themselves. Hence, they could not be connected to other complexes. In this case, their communications with the settlement and external world should be seen as via passages between complexes. The access routing within the complexes in opposite directions testifies that there was no main thoroughfare at this part of the settlement.

At the northwest and southeast parts of the excavation site, 8 buildings and 7 intermediate walls have been located. Because of the bad state of preservation of these sites their plans cannot now be defined.

At Gargalartepesi there are 6 construction layers, only 3 of which contain remains that give us any clues to planning. In the other 3 layers, 5 buildings and 2 intermediate walls have been investigated so far.

The building layer at level 360-300 cm contains the remnants of 8 buildings and 3 intermediate walls (*Fig. 38*). In the centre and southern part of the excavation site there is little evidence of construction. 7 buildings and 1 intermediate wall directly surround a clear area at the site centre. Here, running north/south, are traces of a wall 5.1 m in length. One end joins building 21, but its other end is not revealed. At the middle of the wall there is an access 60 cm wide. On both sides of this access there are traces of small circular structures (diameter 50-55 cm). That this was an important wall is witnessed by its structure, orientation, and the remains of the two circular, tower-like structures. The remains of a hearth have been traced on the western section of the wall, and another beside a wall of building 21. We may take it that the protection afforded from the south by buildings 12 and 21, with the wall laid between them, and the presence of the hearths, implies that the courtyards were to the west of the site walls. Communications from the east of the site to adjacent buildings have not been traced. The main entrances to two buildings lead into opposite areas, and so, the given free site is not a courtyard. It should therefore be regarded as a space for controlling the view from all directions to the entrance of the circular structures (towers). One of the two traced buildings of the complex, building 12, existed over 4 construction layers. Its cylindrical walls remained to layer 210 cm, but no main entrance was noted. This is the sole building with evidence of a pit. All this testifies to the detached character of the given building. In the above interpretation, the complex has a special character, perhaps a spiritual one, given its east-west orientation to the sun.

It should be noted that the latest constructions in this layer are located at a level of 340 cm. Above the 300 cm layer, there was no construction activity. During the accumulation of the 40 cm of cultural layer (at a level of 340-300 cm), there is some stability in the planning and condition of the constructions.

The planning of the construction layer at 300-270 cm, in general, shows a design similar to the previous layer, though out of the 8 buildings from the previous layer, only 4 were retained (*Fig. 39*). At this level only building 12 is saved.

The site free from buildings in this level remains free and shows no signs of construction even at an examined level. Opposite to this site is the exit of new construction 2. Constructions located around the free site, do not bear relation to this site and it is possible to group constructions 20, 15, 16 south of the free site. However these generalizations can be based only on assumptions.

The construction layer at level 270-245 cm, despite its small capacity, differs in its large number of constructions (*Fig. 40*). The plan of the layer consists of 16 buildings and 6 intermediate walls. Of the structures from the previous layer, only building 20 stops here, and, contiguous to it, the wall from the southwest. Building 13 replaces building 20. During its first stage, its exit was to the southeast, i.e. left, to a southern and open site. After reconstruction, this exit was closed and the entrance on the northeast to the central, open area was blocked. This is the only construction that leads directly into this area. On the northwest excavation site there are two new buildings 3 and 11, and two intermediate walls, one of which is laid between them, and the second adjoins to the last, having formed, probably, a courtyard. The access from building 11 leads into this courtyard. To the east, the plan of the complex includes 4 buildings linked by 3 intermediate walls. Here were located buildings 24, 22 (an intermediate wall between them), and 25, which were probably interconnected. The small building 22 has access to the southwest, i.e. into a courtyard. To the east of the site the plan remains constant. The isolated building 18 was deserted at this period and began to decay.

On the results of the excavation, we divided the homogeneous cultural layer of the Chalagantepe settlement into 12 construction layers, at levels: 405-390 cm, 390-370 cm, 370-350 cm, 350-325 cm, 325-305 cm, 305-290 cm, 290-275 cm, 275-255 cm, 255-230 cm, 230-208 cm, 208-190 cm, and above 190 cm (which was much damaged).

The first constructions were created on the natural surface at level 405 cm (*Fig. 6*). Below this mark there are no building remains. The level of the natural surface changes within the 450-400 cm layer. The lowest layer has revealed pits 14, 15, 17, 18, 22, the pit-house 71, buildings 69, 72, 73, 76, 77, 78, 79, and glazing from furnaces 35, 38, 43, 47, and 48. In this layer the character of the plan of the inhabited complexes has not yet been traced. Basically, the constructions are concentrated in the central part of the excavation site. Between buildings 76, 73 and 77 is the rectangular wall that separates the site into two areas, as well as the kilns and pits used for non-domestic functions.

In the following layer (390-370 cm) the remains of dwelling 71, and all pits and furnaces, cease (*Fig. 7*). What remains there are, are from buildings 60, 64, 66, 68, 70, 74, 75, glazing furnaces 34, 37, 39, and pits 13, 20, 21. The plan of this layer shows that the inhabited complexes were contiguous and that the buildings and courtyard were not yet complete. The complex that consists of buildings 79, 76, 77, and the intermediate walls between 76 and 77, has been traced in the southern area. In the northern area there is a section of an intermediate wall, and one may detect a further complex — buildings 74, 68, 66, 73, and an extension of building 77. Between these complexes and buildings there is a passage (1-2 m) running northeast.

The plan of level 370-350 cm basically repeats the plan of the previous layer (*Fig. 8*), and all the constructions of the previous layer continue. In the northern area there are 3 new buildings — 61, 63, 62, but all glazing furnaces remain, and both pits and the extension to building 77, disappear. However, furnaces 32, 41, 42, 45, and pits 16, 19 are created.

At level 350-325 cm, the southern site has been wholly reconstructed (*Fig. 9*). All previous constructions disappear and 12 new buildings are developed — 51, 52, 50, 22, 49, 17, 18, 54, 46, 47, 45, and 53. A group of 11 buildings is located around an open area. Sites free from construction we define as courtyards. With their associated buildings they form a functional unity, or inhabited complex. One such example, in the southern area of the excavation site, we have labelled 'the southern complex'. A further 7 buildings (35, 60, 38, 62, 67, 59, 61, 64) comprise 'the northern complex'.

In the following construction layer (325-305 cm), two complexes from the southern part of the previous layer, and a new complex from the central excavation area, have been traced (*Fig. 10*). This appears to consist of 6 buildings — 10, 35, 26, 28, 40, 65 and a courtyard. The first 4 buildings are located in an arc around the courtyard, and the other two are probably towards the centre of the courtyard. Since the southwest part of the complex has not yet been dug, care must be taken when discussing it. In 3 buildings of the complex there are entrances leading into the courtyard. The condition of the remains, and nature of the fill, indicate the full operation on this level of all 6 buildings.

Significant changes were not detected in the southern complex. There is only building 47, and in place of the destroyed building 54 there is building 23a. In this level, in a destroyed condition, there is a building 50, inside which a glazing furnace was detected. Four furnaces have been traced in the vicinity of the courtyard. Glazing furnaces were short-lived, and consequently it is possible to assume, that the five furnaces of this level existed serially, not simultaneously. Only in one building of this complex were there traces of an opening into the courtyard.

At this level, 7 buildings have been investigated that do not appear to be part of the overall plan. Of these, constructions 51, 55, 56, 38, 39 are of a known type. Building 60 had collapsed and from it only a small part could be traced. Sections of buildings 57 and 43, and a small wall, are connected to buildings 46 and 55.

More significant changes occur at level 305-290 cm (*Fig. 11*) but both complexes retain their overall planning structure. Changes to the central area are insignificant. Alone, construction 26 deteriorates gets at this time, a glazing furnace is created within it and 3 pits have been explored.

In the southern complex both quantitative and qualitative changes occur at this time. Building 45 collapses and is replaced by 19, and building 48 replaces 53. Amid all the changes to building 52, part of the older wall is kept. Buildings 49 and 17 disappear, to be replaced by building 11. Building 23a suffers from some dilapidation. In addition, there are a glazing furnace, pits, and a pit-house on the courtyard site. In spite of all these changes, the general plan of the complex is retained. As well as these two complexes, there are further buildings — 44, 39, glazing furnace 27, 30, 31, pits 9 and 10, and the pit-house 58. From the constructions of the previous layer, building 59, and pits 8 and 11 disappear.

The construction layer at a level 290-275 cm is marked by the revealed outlines of the third complex on the northern part of the settlement (*Fig. 12*). Building 26 is rebuilt and made habitable again, and a part of building 28, forming a border between the central and northern courtyard. But functionally they belong to the central complex, into which courtyard their entrances open. There is another part of a circuit of constructions in the northern complex (buildings 38, 36, 32, 39, 42, 41), located around the courtyard. Some of the constructions of the northern complex existed in the previous layers. With the disappearance of the glazing furnace, and the occurrence here of buildings 36, 32, 42 and 41, the outlines of the courtyard site and its environmental constructions are completed. Only at this level is it possible to speak in detail of the northern inhabited complex. The central complex at this time remains without special changes. As already noted, building 26 is again made habitable at this level. There are also traces of an entrance to building 10 in the southwestern part of the premises; it also leads into the central courtyard.

In the southern complex at this time there are significant structural changes which have not been mentioned. Building 20 replaces the ruined building 50. In addition, building 21 is built on the remains of building 52. Building 46 and the pit-house 1 disappear, to be replaced by building 12, connected to building 23a by an arched wall. Buildings 48, 22, 11, 18, 23a, and 19, continue, allowing the former outline of the courtyard to remain. In the courtyard, 4 glazing furnaces appear, confirming our previous assumption that they existed not simultaneously, but serially.

The construction layer at level 275-255 cm is characterized by the actual decline of the southern complex (*Fig. 13*). Actually the former site of the courtyard remains but is not rebuilt — nor is it protected. In place of buildings 20 and 21 we have building 16, and in a place of building 19, building 14 is under construction. Building 12 continues to exist. From the north, a new building 13 adjoins it. To the west, building 4a is under construction. In the vicinity of the former courtyard, two pits are created. In effect, all the western part of the southern complex has been opened. At this level it is difficult to label it as an inhabited complex. Probably, there was a general, but as yet incomplete, reorganization at this time of the southern complex site.

The central complex at this time remains intact. Two of the complex's constructions, building 40 and 26, receive repair and reorganization. Building 40 is strengthened by the ring which has been added to the socle in a part of a wall. In building 26 same propping up is undertaken internally. At some time an access has also been transferred to the west by a partition constructed inside. In the courtyard a small glazing furnace was added. From what is visible, the planning structure of the central complex at this level remains intact.

In the northern complex only insignificant changes occurred, and only to the southeastern part of the complex. Buildings 41, 42, and 43 cease to exist, and a little bit to the north building 37 constructed — it encroaches, somewhat, on the courtyard, limiting the yard's overall area. At this time, in the centre of the courtyard, a powerful fire takes hold on two fronts. Two circular patches of ash — 70/80 cm — and a further burnt area of 4 sq. m were found. The ferocity and duration of the fire is witnessed by an ash residue of some 10 cm in depth.

The construction layer at level 255-230 cm is characterized by significant reorganization occurring mostly to the southern complex which is now clearly defined and completely planned (*Fig. 14*). Building 13 collapses; 4 buildings are retained and 5 added. They are located in a circle, around a courtyard — traditional planning for a complex such as this. The construction is ordered in such a way that there are three passages to the courtyard. (The southwest one about 1 m wide; the southeast one about 2 m wide; and the east one about 1.5 m wide.).

Many changes took place in the central complex which had remained rather stable in the previous 4 layers. From its southern section, building 2 was added to its arc of construction. Building 34 appears between buildings 26 and 35. Building 26 is dilapidated rather and a glazing furnace is created inside it. The southern extension of building 10 collapses and the construction gets its deserted character. Building 28 is reconstructed.

In the northern complex, re-planning occurs again in the southeast section. Having existed only for short while, building 37 disappears. To the south, buildings 29 and 33 are constructed, between which a direct wall is laid. By these latter constructions, the circle of structures of the northern complex becomes isolated. Of the constructions from the previous layer, buildings 38 and 36 are in a deserted condition. By a wall of building 38 there is a small glazing furnace. In the northern part of the courtyard there is a lavatory, still with its hole of 30-35 cm diameter. It was covered at the top by a thick layer of clay.

The construction layer at level 230-208 cm is the last of the remaining layers (*Fig. 15*). The northern complex has undergone considerable changes in this layer. In place of building 37 (at a level of 275-255 cm), building 31 is under construction. Between it and a retained section of a circle of walls of building 26, is an arched wall dividing the traditional courtyard site. In the northwest half of the courtyard, buildings 36 and 38 (deserted in the previous layer) finally collapse. In place of building 38, building 30 appears. In place of construction 36 are 5 glazing furnaces, also, probably, existing serially. A lavatory hole was also found at this level, after having been sealed by a specially constructed clay dome. In the southeastern half of the courtyard the planning remains without change. There is a single glazing furnace in the courtyard.

The central complex at this level loses its planning integrity because of the dilapidated condition of buildings 28, 26, and 35, and of the complete destruction of building 10. Inside, there are remains still of some of the walls of building 26, building 23; a little to the south building 25 replaces building 10, and building 8 is under construction. As a result of all these changes, especially with the appearance of building 25 in the courtyard area, the outlines of the complex become somewhat obfuscated.

At this level the southern complex keeps its structural planning. The insignificant changes connected to the destruction of buildings 16 and 14, and the new building 15, occur in the southeast section. Others constructions within the complex remain unchanged.

The next two upper layers are much destroyed by modern ground works. The remains left in these layers give no clues as to planning (fig. 16, 17).

On the plans a site may be seen between the northern and southern complexes that continues through 10 layers free from any construction. There are no remains in it consistent with a courtyard site. Most likely it is a site with a greater meaning than simply a courtyard of an inhabited complex. All three traceable inhabited complexes are bound with this site, although the southern complex, in the majority of layers, has no direct passage to this site. Probably it is a courtyard site related to a greater inhabited structure - of an inhabited group consisting of several inhabited complexes. A function of a similar site in an inhabited group should be the maintenance of communication between separate complexes of the inhabited group and communication between the inhabited group and greater settlement. This site could also have held cattle, as the remains in buildings 35, 29, and before testify.

Having considered these 10 preserved construction layers it is possible to detect signs of some distinguishable planning character in the bottom two layers. The intermediate wall of about 9.5 m, opened between buildings 77 and 76, divides two small, inhabited complexes. It is an unusual phenomenon not only for the upper construction layers of the given settlement, but also for the majority of settlements of the given culture. Similar architecture is more characteristic of the Shomutepe settlement, dated 6000 years BC. Hence, the planning structure peculiar for Shomutepe, that basically forms an inhabited complex consisting of 2-3 constructions divided by intermediate walls, is now revealed in the bottom construction layer at Chalagantepe (where it is oldest).

On the basis of an all-round analysis of the above planning construction layers, we may make the following conclusions:

1. For 10 of the construction layers studied, the settlement planning is characterized by the presence of inhabited complexes forming an inhabited group which ultimately forms the whole settlement.

2. The sites of the constructions and courtyards show amazing continuity, proving the strength of the building processes and the presence of spiritual reasons for preserving of the traditional planning structure.

3. Economic activities were undertaken directly in the complex's courtyard, as indicated by the presence of the large number of furnaces, central remains, and pits located in courtyard sites.

4. The arrangement of the constructions around the courtyard and the protective role played by the courtyard, testify to the courtyards' significant functional meaning as the nucleus of an inhabited complex.

The Constructions and their Architecture

Architecturally, constructions are divided into surface type and pit-houses; the pit-houses being the oldest and most widespread type (along with caves), formed in suitable terrain. It is necessary to point out here that the construction of pit-houses did not require any specific terrain surface and this enabled the creation of similar dwellings and settlements irrespective of the relief features of the ground surface itself.

For the flatter areas of Azerbaijan, where little shelter and a lack of building materials are to be found, the pit-house was the most acceptable kind of dwelling. Despite the abundance of pit-houses, they, as well as other kinds of the most ancient dwellings, have been poorly investigated: the relative lack of archaeological material has compounded the situation. More extensive evidence of pit-houses has recently been assembled in Azerbaijan — in particular at Chalagantepe — that allows us to define the architectural features of these kinds of constructions. For the development of any serious work in this direction it is necessary to consider the available archaeological material, analysis of which will allow us to draw some conclusions about their occurrence and development, as well as about the architectural and construction decisions relating to pit-houses in Azerbaijan.

The occurrence of pit-houses as a new type of dwelling should be considered in interrelation with caves and natural shelters of all kinds. The route from cave to pit-house was not a straight line. People living in natural shelters made different adaptations, built artificial protections, carved out niches, holes, even whole caves, and only by developments of this kind did carved out dwellings become actual pit-houses. However such an approach does not provide the basis for us to consider that all pit-houses developed from types of cave shelter. On occasion the earliest pit-houses could have been prototypes for the domestic building of a given region. In this case it is important to trace the 'genetic' connection of the particular culture with more ancient cultures. This will enable us to discover the reasons for this or that type of development for the earliest kinds of dwelling.

The transition from caves to pit-houses was brought about by the discovery of new, more suitable terrains, and quickly established itself as a characteristic of settlement. The reasons for choosing pit-houses included the comparative simplicity of construction and reliability. Pit-houses, with their low roof-lines, were a simple way of coping with the elements. Reliability and simplicity ensured that pit-houses, in many different regions and over several periods (from Neolithic to before antiquity), continued to hold a prominent position among dwelling construction techniques, and did not lose popularity in the subsequent historical periods.

It is impossible to date pit-houses accurately and various assumptions based on today's archaeological data have to be made. However, the data we have on pit-houses from the Mesolithic, for example, makes it possible to interpret some features and draw conclusions when studying dwellings from the Paleolithic.

Architectural features of pit-houses are defined by their layout, design and location within settlements. On investigation, pit-houses may be divided into two basic groups — round and rectangular dwellings. Occasionally we come across pit-houses of a different layout that make single units but are not located in separate groups.

The oldest form of pit-house is the round dwelling. As opposed to other forms, the round type does not seem to have found application in late dwellings and occurs in most cases in Eneolithic settlements. The circular base of the pit-house is most likely explained by its basic simplicity of design and use from a planning perspective, and not by any religious significance.

The development of the planning structure gradually resulted in a transition to a rectangular underground element within the pit-house. In truth, the first rectangular pit-houses differed little from the round type of dwelling. Their corners were rounded, and the walls curved, to some measure features retained in later pit-houses.

The Eneolithic pit-houses were found at the settlements of Baba-Dervish, Alikemektepesi, Chalagantepe, etc. In the literature there is mention of a pit-house at Shomutepe (24; 45, p.106-107). As a result of the careful study of the excavation material there, we surmise that this was a common rubbish pit. The excavator, I.H. Narimanov, writes: "…in this location there is a large, shapeless pit. Probably, the clay extracted from the pit by the Shomutepe inhabitants was used in the construction of brick buildings and the subsequent pit was used for rubbish " (35, p.46). In our opinion this observation does not require further comment.

In the open Eneolithic layer at Alikemektepesi there is a round pit-house dwelling. Its walls are preserved to 45 cm, and were covered with a thick layer of clay painted with white paint, and red ochre drawings (2, p.59).

The large number of pit-houses opened at Chalagantepe distinguishes it from similar Early Eneolithic settlements. In addition, it is the only settlement where the development of pit-houses can be traced through different construction levels and which shows the relationship of pit-houses with raised dwellings. This turns attention to the fact that in the six upper construction layers, pit-houses dwellings have not been traced. They appear in layer 305-290 cm, and at the natural at the level proceeding 405-390 cm. One pit-house was found on the natural below number 71. At 70 cm there were traces indicating that the pit-house was not the first construction in this area. In it was furnace 38, its fuel chamber cut into the foundation pit of the pit-house. To strengthen the foundation pit here, a clay prop, or pilaster, has been fashioned. The floor and walls of the foundation pit were covered with a thick layer of clay, painted wine-red and ochre. Opposite the pilaster to the southwest, a wall adjoins a semicircular platform. The foundation pit was ovoid with vertical sides at 290-310 cm. No raised walls were traced during the excavation.

Pit-house 63 was found at level 363 cm (90 cm up to a level 453 cm). The walls of the foundation pit narrow towards the top by 15-20 cm, so that the diameter at the base of the foundation pit is 3 m, and at the top 2.7 m. The walls and floor are covered with a thick layer of clay that extends over and around the opening of the pit.

In the next construction layer at 350 cm, pit-house 67 was found, ranging from 70 cm to a level at 420 cm; the diameter of its foundation pit was 2.7 m. Pit-house 65 was found in the next layer at 310 cm, ranging from 60 cm to 370 cm. Its diameter was 2.5 m. At the 300 cm level, two pit-houses were found (58 and 1). Both were 40 cm deep and 2 m in diameter.

As can be seen from the above, the 6 lower construction layers contained 6 pit-houses, whereas not one was found in any of the 6 upper layers. In addition, it was noticeable that there was a gradual reduction in percentage terms of the number of pit-houses in relation to the raised or elevated buildings: i.e. on the natural there was 1 pit-house to 5 raised buildings (20 %); at 370-350 cm 1 pit-house to 15 elevated buildings (6.6 %); at 350-325 cm 1 to 22 (4.6 %); at 325-305 cm 1 to 23 (4.4 %); and at 305- 290 cm, 2 to 25 (8 %).

It should be noted that pit-houses were used for all sorts of different purposes (dwellings, non-domestic premises of various kinds, etc.).

The settlements, depending on the form of construction, are divided into three basic groups — settlements with round buildings, settlements with rectangular buildings, and settlements containing both styles. The third group is in turn divided into two subgroups — settlements where round and rectangular constructions coexist in the same building layer, and settlements where these two forms of construction have been found in different construction layers. In the latter case it is necessary to consider separate layers as separate settlements having this or that architectural tradition. In all cases the construction layers with varied architecture cannot have a 'genetic' connection; between these layers there should be seen to be a stratigraphic border. Possessors of the same culture do not exclude the opportunity for various architectural forms to coexist but it is more likely that the distinction of architecture testifies to a distinctive culture.

Geographical analyses of the settlement distribution, with a variety of architecture, show some trend of having round-plan structures in the north, and rectangular ones in the south. It should be noted that, in northern areas, this trend looks indisputable, while for central and southern regions the tradition for rectangular, as opposed to round, constructions predominates. In the area of Lake Urmia, as well as settlements with rectangular buildings, there is a settlement at Yaniktepe that has round buildings. Between the rounded buildings in the north and the rectangular examples in the south, there are monuments and buildings comprising both forms, such as Kultepe 1, Kultepe 2, Ilanlitepe, and Alikemektepesi. These monuments form a connecting strip between the two regions. A variety of architectural forms here possibly suggests simultaneous cultural connections between the two regions.

Settlements with rounded buildings have been investigated unevenly. As well as some typical monuments with round buildings, the settlements at Kultepe 1, Kultepe 2, Alikemektepesi, Ilanlitepe, Baba-Dervish, Garakepektepe, and Guneshtepe have also been explored.

At the Baba-Dervish settlement, a round construction had been excavated on hill 2. Hill 1 has not revealed any elevated constructions but only the remains of their building material which are appropriate to the building material of the constructions on hill 2. Under a Kur-Araz culture level, four round pit-houses from the Late Eneolithic period were found, having diameters of 3-4 m and depths of up to 1 m (29, p.9-11). Investigating hill 1 in the monograph devoted to this monument, G.S. Ismailov does not mention the construction forms (29, p.11-19). In "The Early Bronze Culture of Azerbaijan" he writes, "…it has been established at the Baba-Dervish settlement that the four-cell dwellings were represented by slightly elevated buildings…" (30, p.9). In our opinion, we agree that for one settlement there should be one form of construction — such as hill 2, with its characteristic round buildings. In addition to the special chronological division he creates, the author associates the Baba-Dervish settlement to the first Early Bronze phase, based on his conclusions of round buildings (30, p.32). The author clearly contradicts himself here. Even if he were not familiar with the excavation material of hill 2, the classification system assumes that the form of the constructions should be round.

The Early Bronze layer at Garakepektepe is 7 m thick and is divided into two chronological phases. The bottom layer is characterized by its round-plan buildings. The remains of 7 round constructions, consisting of one area, have been excavated here. They have no extensions. The upper layer provided extremely rectangular buildings, forming a complex of several premises. The Guneshtepe settlement also consisted of round form constructions.

The architectural construction features of these settlements are defined by their round form in the plan, as everything, from individual premises' interiors to settlement layouts as a whole, is subordinate to the given construction form: even the separate distinct and rectangular structures are additional elements of round constructions. At the settlements of Shomutepe, Gargalartepesi, Chalagantepe, and Yaniktepe, distinct and rectangular structures may be viewed as extensions to basic round buildings (or located between them). The separate, rectangular constructions at these settlements are not standardized.

Round constructions have a natural variety of form — from perfectly circular to lengthened ovals. Perfectly circular walls may be ascribed to buildings 25, 27, 10, and 22 at Chalagantepe, buildings 3, 4, 5, 6, 8, and 9 at Shomutepe, buildings 1 and 7 at Toyretepe, and buildings 2 and 4 on hill 2 at Baba-Dervish. In the main, the oval form seems restricted to constructions of non-domestic function. However there are some oval domestic buildings, for example the rather lengthened oval building 32 (ratio of axes 1:1.46) at Chalagantepe. Also oval shaped are buildings 39, 26, 5, 19, 14, 15, and 29 at Chalagantepe, the 3rd and 5th buildings at Shomutepe, building 3 on hill 2 at Baba-Dervish, and buildings 18 and 17 at Gargalartepesi. Buildings of other shapes (besides circular and oval) also exist, and mostly of irregular form (triangles, rectangles, polyhedrons), i.e. buildings 23, 45, 28, and 31 at Chalagantepe, 10, 11, and 6 at Ilanlitepe, 44 at Alikemektepesi, 18 at Gargalartepesi, 4, 15 at Toyretepe, etc. In all these buildings, the corners are strongly rounded, giving a transitional form between circle and polyhedron.

The layout of the separate constructions is extremely simple - a single round space. The walls and the small non-domestic constructions attached to them are so insignificant, that any dwellings having these features may really be considered as single-space dwellings. Exceptionally, with building 26 at Chalagantepe, an attempt was made to separate the structure with a partition wall, however this partition reached only to the middle of the premises and consequently the spatial perception of the overall space has not undergone significant change. The division of round premises into two parts by means of a partition dates only from the Early Bronze Age. At Kultepe 1, buildings 9, 33, and 19 (which has a rectangular extension, 20) have been divided by partitions. Thus, together with its rectangular extension, building 19 consists of three spaces, the functional meaning of which is discussed below. A premises divided into four parts was found in the Early Bronze Age layer at Yaniktepe.

In most cases, the internal spaces of cylindrical buildings were not divided. In terms of design, the internal spaces of round buildings afforded comfortable premises with excellent air circulation, producing a practical microclimate for occupants.

In contrast to the basic constructions, the extensions vary greatly — from a simple wall to multiple premises. The most typical examples have been found at Chalagantepe. The extensions here are associated with buildings 38, 28, 26, 23, 35, 25, 10, 3, 16, and 18. Similar extensions have not been found at Shomutepe. The walls laid between constructions are characteristic of this settlement. In this respect Chalagantepe has more variety, where there are also walls laid between the constructions.

However, extensions with a non-domestic function, being volumetric structures, differ from simple wall-divided courtyards, and Shomutepe, where there are no similar extensions, differs in its simplicity and regularity of construction form. At Gargalartepesi, only one extension (18) is traced (contiguous to building 17 from the northern section). Here too, as at Shomutepe, there were a significant number (10) of intermediate walls. At Toyretepe there are buildings and remains of walls, the uses of which cannot be defined: no extensions have been found, just an insignificant amount of intermediate walling. The bad state of preservation of the Eneolithic constructions at Kultepe 1 does not permit any of their features to be explained with certainty.

In the Early Bronze Age layer at Kultepe 1, the extensions have a form typical of the period. All are rectangular and adjoin basic round buildings. Of these extensions, one only (in annex 20) has fixed walls that form a rectangular premises of approximately 2.5 sq. m. In the other examples there are two walls contiguous to the circular walling of the basic construction. Similar extensions have also been excavated at Yaniktepe. The most typical of these adjoins building 4, its form repeating that of extension 20 at Kultepe 1, but differing in function. At Yaniktepe the extension is on the front, through which it leads into the basic round premises. At Kultepe 1 it creates a third space from two others, divided by a partition of rounded construction. At Yaniktepe, rectangular extensions have also been traced to buildings 12, 13, and 16. Similar extensions have not been uncovered at Garakepektepe and Guneshtepe, where the powerful stone walls of the constructions remain. In similar cases, it is possible that the walls of insignificant extensions made of crude brick or clay would not have survived: it is more likely that they never existed at all.

In the Eneolithic layer at Kultepe 1, round and rectangular constructions have been excavated. The coexistence of these two forms of constructions proceeds at all levels of the 9.2 m Eneolithic layer. The remains of structures at 21.4 m are lowermost. A clay wall (length 2.5 m, width 0.3 m) of a four-cell construction is revealed here. At this depth no other constructions have been found. Above, at 18.8 m, 17.2 m, and 16.15 m, the obvious remains of round-plan constructions have been traced. At levels 16.8 m, 16.45 m, 14.5 m, and 14.3 m, there are remains of straight walls, and only at level 16.15 m were there traces of walls of one rectangular premises. As may be seen, rectangular and round constructions coexisted at all stages of the settlement. Proof of this comes from the remains of rectangular and round constructions opened at level 6.15 m. The author of the excavation, O.A. Abibullaev, writes of the coexistence of both forms of constructions (18, p.36, 38). Regarding the form of construction, Abibullaev, on the basis of a wall at 21.4 m, asserted that in the early period of the settlement there was a rectangular construction form (11, p.33). However, at the end of the excavation (18, p.36) he writes: "The Eneolithic layer basically consisted of round-plan constructions".

Round-plan constructions are of different sizes but they all share common features, irrespective of settlement or culture. The optimum size for each construction depends on several factors - engineering, opportunities of construction technology, functional requirements of buildings, etc. The initial model for ancient farmers and settlers was based on the inhabitants' limited needs. At Eneolithic settlements, therefore, small-scale constructions are in evidence, with diameters approximately 2-3 m. This applies to the settlements at Shomutepe, Toyretepe, Gargalartepesi, and Chalagantepe. An exception is at Kultepe 1, where there are limited remains of diameters 5-8.5 m (18, p.36). Other settlements have revealed construction diameters: 1.5-3.7 m at Shomutepe; 1.2-3.5 m at Toyretepe; 0.65-3.9 m at Gargalartepesi; and 1.3-5.2 m at Chalagantepe.

In the Early Bronze Age, as technical and material opportunities developed, the construction sizes also increased. At Kultepe 1, construction diameters reached on average 5-6 m, with rare exceptions from 3.5-13 m (18, p.80-98). At Guneshtepe the construction diameters exceed 7 m, at Garakepektepe they reach from 3.5-4 m (30, p.9), at hill 2 at Baba-Dervish they reach from 4-4.9 m, at Borispoltepe from 6.5-7 m, and at Yaniktepe from 4-8 m.

There are difficult questions about the origins of the new architectural tradition, i.e. the appearance of round-plan buildings. In various areas of the Near East and adjacent regions, both traditions (rectangular and round-plan constructions) are present from deepest antiquity (Pre-ceramic Neolithic and even Mesolithic). Advanced rectangular constructions are well known at Erihon B, pre-ceramic Hajilar, Chayonu Tepesi, Jarmo, and Tel

Magzalia. Round constructions in significant numbers are known from Eynan (10-9th millennium), Erihon A (late 9th-8th millennium), Mureybit, Beyd, Ganj-Darekh, etc. (17). In the Eneolithic period round-plan architecture was widely adopted in the territories adjacent to the Southern Caucasus (Halaf culture), but in none of the earliest agricultural cultures of the Near East has round-plan architecture of such an organic, unadulterated nature as that of the South Caucasus been uncovered.

Further afield, if we take in all round-plan constructions, the distribution area is extensive. To the west it includes Mersin in Anatolia, to the east, similar constructions have been excavated on the Dekan peninsular; to the north it reaches into the Northern Caucasus, and to the south as far as Mesopotamia.

It becomes apparent that the Southern Caucasus, in particular Azerbaijan, is at the centre of the culture of round-plan buildings. This circumstance requires special attention, as the architectural study of the round-plan buildings of Azerbaijan can most directly assist our investigation of this culture. One might even go so far as to say that the study of the round-plan buildings of Azerbaijan might provide a general solution to the question of the origin of this architectural tradition.

It is important to emphasize that more than two-thirds of the 150 settlements of this culture investigated in the Southern Caucasus are in the territory of Azerbaijan (36, p.4). If we take into account the fact that fixed monuments represent an insignificant number of all existing settlements, one may be reasonably confident in placing Azerbaijan among the likely centres of this architectural tradition.

As against settlements in the northern areas of Azerbaijan, the settlements of the central and southern areas are characterized by rectangular buildings. They have been excavated in construction layers 1 and 2 at Alikemektepesi, at Ilanlitepe, Leylatepesi, in the Eneolithic layer of Kultepe 1, and in the upper construction layers of the Early Bronze Age periods at Garakepektepe.

Decision-making and the constructions; reconstructions

The architecture of the Eneolithic period is known for its use of clay. At this time, all the environmental elements of settlements — courtyards, constructions, interior elements, and the majority of household objects were made of clay, a widely available material. At the beginning of a settlement, where the first structures were built on the natural, clay was taken from holes dug out near to the building platform. With an increase in the cultural layer, these holes for clay had to be dug further afield, probably on its perimeter, thereby creating a trench around the settlement. Subsequently these holes were used for different non-domestic purposes, e.g. for the disposal of ashes and debris.

In the construction process, clay was used from different holes, and consequently one construction could possibly contain different colour bricks and coatings; vegetative impurities in manufacture would vary the texture and elasticity of the bricks. (Bricks without organic impurities are found. Such bricks tend to appear at the foundation level and within the reorganization of walls.)

The bricks are lengthened rectangles with convex upper surfaces ('plain convex' type)(*Fig. 24*). The sizes of the bricks are not standard — not even from construction to construction. However, all the 'plain convex' type retain their basic rectangular form with convex upper surfaces. Analyses of bricks show a uniformity of proportion that can be expressed as a ratio of 4:2:1. This shows that, despite the different sizes, certain standards were adhered to in brick manufacture. The freest of the three dimensions was the first. This is understandable because, given the technology in use, when the walls were under construction, brick length had little influence on design. On average, the lengths of bricks varied between 35-40 cm, with fluctuations from 25 cm to 55 cm. Brick width depended on the thickness of the walls. Depending on the function of the construction, the bricks were produced to a certain width. It is necessary to note that the width of bricks of one construction were more or less equal, with a variance of not more than 5%. The most standard width is around 18 cm — with some fluctuation between 10-25 cm. The third brick measurement — height — also had a mean standard, 9 cm, with fluctuations from 7-14 cm. Some constructions demanded a standardized brick height; especially important for certain brickwork features.

It is difficult to be precise regarding brick manufacture. The faces of the round and rectangular bricks are not always straight and parallel. Some curved bricks were inserted to form circular wall. As well as these, there were bricks of the lengthened-oval form. Apparently, the processes for manufacturing and drying bricks were undertaken in areas close to the foundations; the bricks may have been dried on sand and ash, as traces of these materials have been found on them. Fired bricks have been found: some of them closed an entrance aperture of building 69 at Chalagantepe, and some were located in the wall courses of building 29 at Alikemektepesi (4, p.16). In our opinion, these bricks were not fired especially for construction purposes, but were occasionally fired in kilns intended for ceramics, and overlapping in the chamber caused variation in surface patterning (as at Chalagantepe).

On hills 1 and 2 at Baba-Dervish, constructions were created from crude bricks, rods, branches and canes. On some floors of buildings on hill 2 there were remains of branches near crude walls. Hill 1 had no traces of actual constructions, but one layer did reveal fragments of clay 2-8 cm thick, on which there were impressions of cane rods, as well as pieces of crude bricks (29, p.12-13).

Some sites do retain foundations of clay and brick constructions. At Kultepe 1 (18) there are cobbles set in clay, combined with the bases of construction walls. The upper parts of the walls of these constructions are built of solid clay. A layer at Geytepe (on the western shore of lake Urmia) contains stone bases combined with brick walls of rectangular constructions. The tradition continued there into the Early Bronze Age period of layer B (12. p.17-20, 34-36). Stone bases are also found in Early Bronze Age layers at Kultepe 1, Kultepe 2, Guneshtepe, Garakepektepe, Baba-Dervish hill 2, etc.

At Early Bronze Age Garakepektepe, both round-based and rectangular constructions were found, made from stone fragments, flattish bricks, and small cobbles set in a clay mix. The floors and inside walls were covered with clay, and the round buildings were covered with red paint. At Guneshtepe, the construction walls were made of larger stones. Here again the inside walls were covered with a thick layer of clay (30, p.8-9).

The design of elevated constructions differs significantly from pit-house (rounded) dwellings, the main features being platform, base, and wall. In discussing such constructions, separate consideration should be given to each design element. Most interesting, and most debatable, are questions relating to the design of round-plan constructions. Over the last 40-50 years there has been much controversy and many questions remain unanswered. One such question concerns the form and design of the roofing of these constructions — in most cases no traces of the method or means of roofing remain.

The study of most ancient architecture is closely connected with archaeological excavation. Experts engaged with the theoretical questions of architecture have to rely for their conclusions on the published results of archaeological excavations in which it is not always possible to trace design features of the constructions revealed. As a result, there are several reconstruction projects which deviate from set architectural rules.

On the basis of personal experience at certain archaeological excavations it is possible to reveal the basic design and architectural features of the constructions of the Eneolithic period. To do so, it is necessary to analyze the construction processes and, if applicable, their subsequent destruction and rebuilding phases over time.

In the Eneolithic period, the constructions had features consistent with current building materials and appropriate technologies. One of these features was building without the use of foundations, i.e. buildings were built directly on the ground, or on the levelled remains of previous constructions. The absence of foundations did not mean that builders did not know, or understand, the importance from a stability point of view of this design feature. The levelled platforms on which constructions were built were relatively stable bases. Even settlement areas previously used for clay working provided good construction platforms. Stone bases have been traced at Kultepe 1, Baba-Dervish hill 2, Guneshtepe, Garakepektepe, etc. Similar bases, constructed of one row of flat stones, are known from both the Eneolithic and Early Bronze Age layers of Kultepe 1.

Above a base platform, or directly on the ground, the floor of a construction was raised slightly above the ground, on a level with the courtyard. This feature has been described by O.A. Abibullaev (18) at Kultepe 1. The same opinion is held by the authors of the excavations at Yarimtepe, who assert that: "evidence has not been found which might indicate the presence of deep footings dug especially for constructions.

As a rule, the constructions were built directly on to a surface that had probably been levelled previously" (34, p.190). After preparation of a suitable 'platform', a ring of walls was built to a low height, and then the inside was filled with clay, so creating the floor base. Some authors believe that the floor was always 30-50 cm below the level of the courtyard. They describe the preliminary preparation of a shallow pit, in which the lower walls were then covered, backfilling the bottom of the construction, which was then levelled when the construction was finished (28, p.21). The statement that the floors were below the courtyard is accurate, but it has more to do with the floors of a previous construction. The new construction was built on a flat area, or on a platform, hence the floor could not be below the courtyard. Where a construction was built directly on the ground, or on a base, the clay floors could be up to 20 cm thick. Therefore the floor of the new construction could appear to be 20 cm above the level of the courtyard. Subsequently, as the courtyard layers increased, the floor of the premises gradually appeared lower than the level of the courtyard. In buildings that existed over a long period, the floor appeared much lower than the level of the courtyard. When this discrepancy reached 30-50 cm, the floor of the premises was raised to a new level. Excavations show that the floors of the constructions rose repeatedly. At Chalagantepe, a rise in floor level of up to 70 cm was observed.

The buildings at Haji Firuz, and on the small hill at Yaniktepe, have powerful walls coated with a thick layer of gypsum (14, p.138). The overlapping was probably flat and the ends of the supporting beams were put on the longer walls. In similar buildings there are indoor walls contiguous to the longer walls. They were undoubtedly a construction feature that increased the stability of the walls and overall rigidity of design, but they did not serve in any way to support the overlapping beams. There was an optimum width for the overlapping, and the beam ends were better located on firm walls rather than on a central supporting beam. The advantages of long platforms are few, and cannot be justified in terms of construction effort.

At Alikemektepesi there are brick piers by the inside corners that have also been thought of as roof supports. These features seem to have been added during the construction phase of building 39 (2, p.55). Piers of two rows of bricks were first erected in the corners, and then a further row was attached to them from the external parts of the walls. Similar angular piers are found in other buildings and at lower layers. These features may also be thought of as design elements for the walls. Additional design elements were reed roofs and coatings of special waterproof clays.

Fragments of clay with cane imprints (once parts of roofs) have been found in similar buildings at Alikemektepesi. At different layers within building 8 the remains of burnt reeds have been found (2, p.56-57). The nature of the finds gives rise to the suggestion that they had fallen from the roof. The pattern of the reed finds, at different levels of the fill, testifies to the duration of the destruction process and the gradual filling-in of the construction.

On the floor of building 54 are the remains of matting. Above this floor (10-15 cm) the fill contained fragments of matting and reed which had also undoubtedly fallen from the ceiling (5, p.5). The floor of building 40 was covered with matting at 270 cm and, at 250-265 cm, its fill also contained traces of matting and reed (2, p.56-57).

At Ilanlitepe a construction was found whose walls consisted of one and two rows of bricks. One row of bricks was combined with the basic wall of the smaller building. Inside the premises the walls had brick piers which might also have had a structural significance. Here, as well as at other settlements, the brick piers acted as buttresses for strengthening the walls, and assisting with the roofing structure.

The excavator at Khizaanat-Gora has reconstructed some of the buildings there using a flat overlapping technique based on a structural pier (28, p.144). The author observes that the piers were not present in all buildings. For some rectangular constructions at Kvatskhela, the author suggests flat overlapping in ring form, in two or three tiers. He also remarks that in the middle of the structure there was a circular aperture for letting in light and extracting smoke. He also observes: "a pier freely installed in the middle of the main premises…" (28, p.124). In actual dimensions, the diameter of the beams used would have been about 15-20 cm, and the supporting piers about 30-40 cm. The author goes on to report that the beams were occasionally doubled (28, p.128). Such massive beams would have been unnecessary for overlaps of only 3 m. The author also states that the piers were thicker towards the top. If they reached a diameter of 30-40 cm below, it is unclear what size they would have needed to be at the top. The braided, clay-covered walls — a feature of this settlement — would have been unable to support such a heavy design.

Rather early on at Yaniktepe 1, there is evidence of the distribution of buttresses — that characteristic building feature that subsequently plays such a significant role in Shumer architecture. Buttresses seem to have been employed throughout the existence of the settlement (34, p.70), and this must have been to strengthen walls both inside and out. The excavators at Hassuna have made similar findings (16. p.273). The explanation of the term buttress in these applications refers to "the semicircular ledges found on the long walls, to which a beam that crossed the centre of the room was fixed" (16. p.273). As a variant, longer party walls had pairs of buttresses, because in order to cover the space not less than three crossbeams would have been required. The roofing method suggested by the authors is unlikely to have satisfied the builders.

The walls of the constructions were assembled mostly from one line of crude bricks arranged lengthways. The brickwork was mortared by a clay solution, usually 1.5-2 cm thick. Separate buildings had special styles of brickwork. The walls of building 2 at Chalagantepe, and some constructions at Ilanlitepe, are marked by their angular arrangement of bricks (37, p.10). The corners of the bricks projected outwards, thus creating wall surfaces that aided the fixing of roofs and increased thickness. The same effect is found at building 26 at Chalagantepe, where a complicated bricklaying technique was employed in both interiors and exteriors of certain constructions. Similar brickwork has also been found within the Early Bronze Age layer of Kultepe 1 (18, p.82). The walls of building 16 used a method of brickwork that afforded a considerable saving of bricks. At Toyretepe, a wall of building 4 is made of two rows of bricks - one lengthways and the other placed across it. The width of this wall reaches 40 cm. At Shulaveris-Gora, the brickwork of the wall of a small round structure featured crude bricks placed ends up (28, p.21). The Eneolithic layer of Kultepe 1 retained the stone bases of some constructions and some few remains of clay walls. The Early Bronze Age layers had similar remains, but this layer also contained some brick constructions (18, p.81). The basic differences of wall design over the different periods relate primarily to their relative strengths. The constructions of the Early Bronze Age had powerful walls that could reach up to 70 cm in height. Alikemektepesi featured some clay constructions, but brickwork featured significantly in the building processes (2, p.56).

The constructions' walls, made as described above, were coated with a thick layer of clay. This clay coating was restored regularly, and it could reach a thickness of 15 cm at the bases of the walls. At Chalagantepe, the walls of building 26 had three internal coating layers, each of a thickness of 1.5-2 cm (*Fig. 25*). At a later stage a further coat was added, with a maximum thickness at the bottom of 5-7 cm. Externally, the coatings were also regularly reapplied. These outside walls were also coated to the very base of the walls, sometimes reaching a thickness of up to 40 cm. In cases where less brickwork was employed, the clay coating was still applied. The coating not only afforded stability, but also allowed for a certain architectural expressiveness. Monotonous brickwork did not always lend itself to design detailing and so the builders used clay and clay coatings to create form. This may be seen on the remains of the walls of the entrance to building 29, the end face of a partition within building 26 at Chalagantepe, and the entrance walling to buildings 5 and VII at Shomutepe.

The weakest area of any wall was at ground level: the complex pressures in play explain the reason. To tackle this the builders were forced to strengthen this part of the walls with a thick coating that effectively sealed the point of contact of the wall with the ground. This coating also protected the walls from water and promoted wall stability, rather than "balancing radial effort" as some authors believe (28, p.20). This rounded coating at the base of the walls (sometimes thick, sometimes thin) is found at most construction sites.

Walls coated on both sides with such care resulted in monolithic cylinders with some rigidity of design. Buttresses added further stability. Typical examples are found with building 1 at Toyretepe. These were formed transversely by the bricks laid in three piers against the walls. These piers have remained in places to a height of 120 cm. Smaller examples have been found in constructions at Chalagantepe. Here, two walls have been strengthened by such a feature, as well as three entrance apertures. At Shomutepe no buttresses have been found. Here, at only one location was a wall strengthened by transverse brickwork, but walls laid between buildings have been traced. Each construction is attached by 1-3 similar walls, creating a rigid design. Shomutepe, therefore, did attempt some form of stability featuring.

The remaining entrance apertures were small, with widths of up to 80 cm and residual heights of up to 50 cm. The small aperture of building 26 at Chalagantepe is 47 cm wide and with a remaining height of 44 cm. Taking into account the widths of other entrance apertures (especially that of building 28, with a width of 80 cm), it is possible to imagine that the entrance apertures could have been quite high (*Fig, 22, 23, 25*).

As mentioned above, the walled constructions represent monoliths. The apertures were not designed to influence durability, but they did, nevertheless, act as buttresses of a kind. At Shomutepe, the thickening of walls and aperture thresholds have been detected in buildings 5 and VII. At Chalagantepe, 3 of the 5 entrances have been similarly strengthened. Building 14 at Gargalartepesi has an inside diameter of 40 cm, and its aperture size is 15 cm (9, p.7). This size of aperture quite corresponds to the dimensions of a cylindrical construction, and also, probably, to its situation. Some apertures have heel-stones or depressions in the ground which are indicative of doors. Similar entrances have been found in the Eneolithic layer of Kultepe 1 — in building 5 at level 14.5 m (18, p.35). A straight wall, 4 m in length, has been uncovered here, constructed of two rows of cobblestones and filled with clay. The wall ends at a cone-shaped stone with a small indentation. A similar stone was found at Leylatepesi, allowing for a door arc of 70°. At Ilanlitepe, the aperture of building 11 had a width of about 1 m. In the earth was a depression 15 cm in diameter and 20 cm deep (39, p.7). It suggests that there was a door post here.

Study of the actual material remains of these round-plan structures presents enough data to allow us to speculate on their form and design. The method of roofing still poses many questions: the only evidence comes from what may be deduced from other construction elements. The buildings themselves, as we have seen, are round-plan, with cylindrical walls and a small entrance aperture. Each such construction has, in effect, its own structural and aesthetic coordinates, and, therefore, the roofing should correspond to the other elements of the design. Each design has its own laws dictated by necessity, and studying any construction by its remains means understanding the necessity incorporated within the basics of a particular design. In considering each architectural element one must uncover the design rationale behind it.

The first problem to consider is that relating to the roofing of those constructions that have no traces of a central supporting post. Elsewhere, we have commented on the necessity for an efficient and easy method of roofing to accommodate the readily changeable walling process. Before detailing the roofing method in this model, it is necessary to consider some alternative variants. In the Eneolithic period, when metal tools were only just developing, processing thick logs in the quantities required for roofing materials was very difficult, if not impossible. In those buildings that show no traces of central posts, the roofing could be flat, but the weight would have been too great for the walls and some sort of crude brick dome shape would have evolved. However, the remains of the walls show no traces of doming, and, most probably, the walls were always vertical. Building 12 at Gargalartepesi would have had walls 2 m in height, and these are absolutely vertical. The same vertical positioning applies for all the constructions at Chalagantepe. At Gadachriligora, A.I Javakhishvili writes about a significant narrowing to the upper walls and he states that he found "a crude building with an almost complete dome" (28, p.73). The same author, writing about the buildings at Shulaveris-Gora, describes them as "... being constantly updated ...Building 3 has been constantly added...to the 2 metre...spanning 400 to 700 years" (31, p.31). It is not clear whether the dome of the building could have been raised. It would have been possible to raise the walls, but only by removing the dome and this does not seem feasible. The author marks the presence above the door aperture of faint traces of wooden cross posts, logically considering them: "as temporary supports for the brickwork while the mortar was hardening" (28, p.21). These ancient builders did not know the arch and could not have built one above a 50 cm door aperture, let alone have constructed brick domes with a diameter of up to 5 m.

At Shomutepe the archaeological excavation reports detail the walls of building 5, with a diameter 2.1 m, which remain to a height of 62 cm, rising gradually and narrowing inside. The (non-domestic) building number 6, with a diameter of 2.1 m, has each row of bricks overlapping inside by 6-10 mm. The walls rise to 105 cm, gradually narrowing (8, p.2, 15). The author does not quantify the incline at the height of 105 cm. Taking into account the dimensions of the bricks (7-8 cm) and thickness of the mortar solution (about 2 cm), it is possible to calculate this narrowing: - 6-10 mm x 1050 mm / 70-80 mm + 20 mm = 88 mm. This calculation shows that in a construction with a diameter of 2.1 m, it is impossible to have overlapped and sloping walls. In addition, the reports discuss cylindrical detached structures, including building 7, which remained to a height of 90 cm (7, p.4). These cylindrical constructions are also noted by some Georgian researchers (31, p.1-10). However the majority of researchers, not fully acquainted with the excavations, all opt for the erroneous concept of dome construction. As a result, even such fundamental works as "Eneolithic USSR" (Volume 4 in "Archaeology USSR"), contain incorrect information on Shomutepe - for example by describing a structure as a: "…domed figurative construction with overlapping dome …" (45, p.106).

Erroneous concepts are not limited to the question of round-plan roof covering. They extend to nearly all aspects of design, from building materials to volumetric-spatial decisions. For example, A.I. Javakhishvili is confused by the absence of brick remains and will not admit the possibility of clay overlap with diameters of about 6 m. Consequently he considers that the basis for design was a wooden framework (28, p.149). In response, it is not clear why it is possible to build a 6 m diameter of crude brick, but not one of clay mass, when we see no basic difference between these two materials. Secondly, there may be no brick remains, but neither are there any remains of frameworks. The reasons for choice are not clear in this case. Javakhishvili writes: "…the elliptical plan more often applies to larger dwellings, and is probably explained by a desire to increase stability…" (28, p.22). Right away we can point to building 60 at Chalagantepe; it has a diameter as wide as 5.2 m, and is perfectly circular. There are similar parallels at Shomutepe, Gargalartepesi, Toyretepe, etc. As regards the question of partitions, it is necessary to note that, because of the non-uniform distribution of stresses on the walls, the elliptical plan far from raising stability actually weakens it. Javakhishvili goes on to assert that, at Toyretepe, and with building 8 at Imiris-Gora, wall pilasters provide rigidity for the edges of domed constructions. He also explains the reason for their occurrence by an increase in the size of premises (28, p.87). As already stated, there are buildings at Toyretepe with a diameter of 3.4 m. (building 1), as well as a larger building with a diameter of 5 m (building 21). The same large constructions have been found at other settlements, including Shulaveris-Gora, about which the author also writes. There were no fixed posts in any of them, indicating that such posts were not connected to any increase in construction sizes. As for: "providing rigidity for the edges of domed constructions", it is possible to say with confidence that, at Toyretepe, the constructions had vertical walls and any transition towards doming has not been traced. The Toyretepe researcher writes that: "the walls of building 1 were vertical and stood to a height of 120 cm" (42, p.19-20). The idea of an edged dome covering has no scientific validity. On page 64 of the study, the author goes on to suggest that the two round building 9-10 were joined by a flat overlapping roof. At Imiris-Gora, buildings 8, and 9-10 are located beside each other: building 9-10 sharing the eastern partition of building 8 which preceded it. Both are also stylistically close in planning terms, consisting of two contiguous round premises. Despite these similarities, the author interprets them differently. Our conclusion is that Imiris-Gora, so characteristic of an extensive Shomutepe-culture settlement, had vertically walled structures. This is proposed by the author for building 9-10, but there was no evidence of flat overlapping for this construction. A settlement, of course, was not a place for arbitrary architectural experimentation: construction at this time had its traditions, from which one may determine which culture it belonged to, and its chronological framework. To expect such a variety of architectural features in one settlement is the equivalent of expecting Kur-Araz ceramics to be found with Hassuna material! Further, on page 88, the author writes: "...there is only one fact: that the buildings are round-plan, which presupposes that they had overlapping domes..."

Y.K Amirjanov went further in his investigation of Kultepe 1: "...Those round-plan buildings that had no trace of retaining stones for wooden posts that propped up the roof, were of 'false-dome' design" (23, p.101). For example the combination of the crude brick building 34 (7.3m diameter) and clay building 4 (6.4 m diameter). According to the author, those structural remains that had a central post had: "vertical cylindrical walls and a flat roof" (23, p.101).

Thus, there are no convincing arguments for the benefits of overlapping brick or clay domes. But a case can be made for two probable overlapping variants that we have studied and modelled. The first is applicable for smaller constructions, with a diameter of up to 1.5 m which could be covered by a roof that needed no supporting feature. Such overlapping could be fashioned from reeds, fastened into an inverted cone and plaited in several circular sections. Such cone-figured overlapping could be created from matting and would have been an effective covering.

For larger buildings, overlapping coverings that had no internal supporting features, during the process of extending the base, would not have been secure. To cope with vertical stresses, such a design would require a central post, and the majority of excavations have not revealed these. The support feature we propose is that the beams rested along the length of the base as well as on the circular walls themselves, thus forming a polyhedron. If this were the case, the dimensions of the beams could be decreased, and, unlike with the usual flat overlapping process, the beams could possibly be swapped for branches, or even large reeds. Therefore, the superimposed polyhedrons gradually narrow in diameter as the layers rise. The end result is a rigid, overlapping domed structure. At the same time, the construction was transportable and could be readily dismantled and rebuilt. The circular aperture left in the centre of the covering did not materially affect the durability of the design. The aperture could easily be covered by mats, reeds, etc.

The studies of the structural remains at Shomutepe, Toyretepe, Gargalartepesi, and Chalagantepe enable us to assert that all the constructions at these settlements developed similarly in terms of design. There are some exceptions, however, and these will be considered separately.

On hill 2 at Baba-Dervish, two of the three surviving constructions show depressions caused by posts where the walls met the ground. These depressions are found 45 cm - 80 cm apart. Building 3 had 7 of these and building 2 had 5 (*Fig. 45*). The structural details allow us to develop a distinct design for the walls and overlapping. It is very clear that the depressions located on the perimeter of the walls were created by posts. As mentioned above, posts were unlikely to aid wall stability, and so their use for this purpose here is excluded. They are more likely to have been employed as a type of rafter, used as an overlapping support structure able to carry the entire roofing load. These buildings probably started with an outline frame or skeleton that could have accommodated the cone-shaped, or domed, covering. The latter seems more probable as the remains show that the lower wall sections include bricks. Up to a certain height, brick walls would be vertical, and only converge into a dome shape towards the top. More than likely, the upper parts of the walls were not bricks, but clay. In similar designs, the posts of the frames interlock with opposing uprights, and these determine the height of the structure: a reasonably rigid dome results, and one that could be covered with different materials. The lower vertical walls could be brick. The design enabled spaces to be left for the entrance and smoke extraction, and these would not reduce the stability of the overall design. Where central retaining posts are used this design is unnecessary. Despite this, there is a post-hole in building 3. Posts used in these designs might well have had auxiliary functions, bearing some of the vertical stress itself. The post helped reduce some of the total stresses at work on the skeleton frame and walls.

The earliest examples of a similar design may be seen in the Zagros mountains, in the Neolithic settlement of Zavi Chemi (dated 10-9th millennium BC), where there are open, rounded constructions with stone bases and walls with wattle and clay (33, p.23). There are also very ancient constructions at Neolithic Erihon-A (9-8th millennium BC) - round-plan buildings in crude brick. There are no posthole remains in the ground, but the reconstruction is based on overlapping, with a curved structure of bound rods covered with clay (33, p.35).

Settlements of round-plan buildings have been found with posthole impressions in the ground - building 6 at Shomutepe (8, p.13), building 12 at Gargalartepesi (9, p.12), and building 3 at Baba-Dervish. A unique example is at Kultepe 1, where there is one hole in building 2 of the Eneolithic layer and flat stones in buildings 28, 18, 10, and 7 (18, p.27-35). Elsewhere, in the badly preserved Eneolithic layer at Kultepe 1, a site with seven postholes indicates how other constructions in the settlement might have looked. In the Early Bronze Age layer there are rounded buildings whose centres can be traced by a series of flat stones on which central posts once stood (or which marked the positions of partitions that replaced the central pole). Hence, constructions from both cultural layers at Kultepe 1 employed a design based on overlapping and employing a central post. The importance of the central post is confirmed by the presence of postholes carefully laid with cobblestones. Such a posthole can be noted at level 16.45 m, with a diameter of 15 cm, and 60 cm deep (18, p.31). A similar hole is visible in the Early Bronze Age layer at Kultepe 2. Here the hole was dug first and then lined with a flat stone; a post of 30 cm diameter was then placed in the hole.

Similar forms of construction are found at Elar, Shengavit, and Kosi-Koter. The researchers of these monuments, as well as the excavator at Kultepe 1, consider these structures to have been overlapped and conical (40, p.172; 41, p.32; 43, p.152; 44, p.157; 18, p.102). At Yaniktepe, postholes were not found in all buildings, and this prompted C. Burney to suggest a reconstruction using a braided framework covered with matting and clay (13, p.238). We may propose a similar reconstruction for hill 2 at Baba-Dervish, where postholes were similarly not discovered in all the buildings. However, our example had to take into account the remains of posts, set in the walls, which were not present at Yaniktepe. The central flat stones were also found in two of the seven round constructions at Garakepektepe (30, p.9).

The basis of the overlapping design was a central post and rafters. The post was driven into the ground and rested on a flat stone. The height of the post was always above the walls; the higher the roofing the better the water dispersal off it. The rafter ends were attached to the central post, probably interlinking, and to the walls. For stability it was necessary to fix them to at least three separate locations around the circle of walls. Where the central post was driven hard into the floor (as opposed to being placed in a hole), the stability of the design was increased and it was unnecessary to fix the rafters. However, in those designs where the post was set in a hole, on a stone core, it was necessary to increase stability by securing rafters to the central post and walls. A space could usually be left under the roofing to allow smoke to escape and prevent precipitation from entering. Roofing materials would have included reeds, matting, straw, skins, etc.

The functions of constructions

From their cultural and design features, the character of the constructions may be divided into two basic groups - those constructions used as dwellings and those used for other purposes. It has to be noted that the condition of the remains does not always allow us to make an obvious distinction. Dwellings are determined, first of all, by their central layouts, which differed from those structures used for storing food and other materials. These latter structures contained the remains of large containers that would have been used for storing grain, etc. As well as these main constructions, furnaces for glazing ceramic products have been found, as well as pits for different purposes.

At Chalagantepe, some rather well preserved dwellings and non-dwellings have been investigated. The most interesting of these is building 26 which at different times was used as a dwelling. It began at level 325 cm, and its primary floor and wall base are also at this level. At this period, the dwelling consisted of one oval space with a diameter of 2.3-2.6 m. The entrance aperture is 38 cm above the floor which was covered with dark-grey clay and sloped 10 cm to the north. The floor had no apparent remaining features (i.e. a central post hole). However, taking into account the ash covering, it is possible to assume that the centre area was destroyed by holes dug subsequently. After the first inhabitation period the construction was abandoned and furnace 19 built inside; part of the foundation pit hearth cut into the floor of the dwelling. At this time the overlapping, and some of the walling, was destroyed - reorganization at a level of the subsequent floor is very evident to the northwest. The new floor corresponds to the secondary inhabitation phase of the premises, when it once again becomes a dwelling. The floor consists of pure yellow clay, 10 cm thick in the south and 20 cm thick in the north; thus the gradient of the floor to the south is increased. Three different central spaces have been discovered, one of which is 5 cm in depth. Towards the northern wall a vessel was found in the floor. This vessel seems to have had some permanent function within the dwelling space. The level of the floor in front of the entrance is 23 cm below the threshold, and did not necessitate the reorganization of the entrance. However, the habitable phase for any premises is short before needing some sort of repair or restoration. The above floor was totally covered with ashes 5-6 cm thick, and at this layer a new floor was formed from yellow large-granular clay, 2-5 cm thick. This floor, in turn, did not last for long. Three holes were subsequently dug in it, all cutting through to the bottom layers of the premises, indicating that the dwelling was again abandoned at this time. The next inhabitation phase of the premises is connected to a further reorganization and repair of the construction. The northern (dilapidated) part of the walling was strengthened by an internal retaining wall (residual height 20 cm, and width 25 cm). The space is partially divided by a partition leading from the entrance, creating a type of corridor and thus lending the structure a sophistication that distinguishes it from earlier dwellings. The walls at this time were painted white and drawn on with red paint. Two fragments of the painted surface remained on the partition. More layers of the coating, in places up to 15 cm thick, were then applied. After this final phase, the remains of the premises were again reused for a glazing furnace 13.

Building 28 adjoins building 26 from the west: the dwelling consists of one oval space (diameter 245 - 265 cm). Both constructions are located simultaneously at level 325 cm. The lowest floor of the construction is flush with the base of the walls. The floor in places is 3 cm thick. The floor inside is at 322 cm. The entrance aperture in the southern wall is at is 3 cm thick. The floor inside is at 322 cm. The entrance aperture in the southern wall is at level 247 cm, i.e. 75 cm higher than the floor. The upper section of the entrance no longer remains, but taking a probable width of 85 cm, the aperture itself must have been high. The entrance was utilized over the three phases of the dwelling, as expressed by the three different floor levels at 322 cm, 292 cm, and 272 cm. At level 246 cm there was evidence of reconstruction, and in the course of realignment the west section of the walls was destroyed. At reconstruction, this part of the wall was extended outwards by 60 cm, but the other sections of the walls were unchanged: the reorganization demonstrates continuous habitation. The floor of this period should have been at a level corresponding with the base of the new wall, i.e. at level 246 cm, however, except for the remains of matting on the threshold at this level, there were no traces of a corresponding floor. The previous entrance at this time became redundant and the new one was probably located higher up, on a section of wall that has now disappeared. Building 28, therefore, was used as a dwelling over 3-4 periods, and, with building 26, formed one inhabited complex. The entrances of both dwellings lead into the courtyard of this complex.

The third dwelling in this complex is building 10; its original floor level was found at level 320 cm. The entrance aperture of this period (50 cm wide) is on the northern section, 25 cm higher than the floor. The floor revealed the remains of two hearths. The first - towards the east wall - was at a depth 12 cm. It was oval shaped, 15-20 cm in diameter, and with clay-covered sides. The second hearth was found on the opposite side towards the western wall. Its remains were found 35 cm from the wall. At a later phase (at level 310 cm, i.e. at 10 cm above the original building) two additions were made. One, a lengthened oval, adjoins from the south, and the other, a straight wall adjoins, from the east. For stability, it was strengthened at both ends by posts. The oval extension was obviously not a dwelling, and more than likely its original design never reached the full height of the dwelling. The rectangular extension could have acted as a windbreak, especially since the remains of the hearth were found at its base.

One of the larger constructions at Chalagantepe was the storehouse, building 1 (3 m in diameter), found at level 240 cm. Inside were found three large vessels, two with diameters of 75 cm and one 100 cm in diameter (*Fig. 14*). The vessels were situated in the lowest floor level at 30 cm, and, undoubtedly, were intended for grain storage. The certain attribution of function to building 1 allows us to be on our guard when it comes to ascribing dwellings to larger constructions and non-dwellings to smaller ones; here there are non-dwelling units of distinctly varying sizes. It would be more accurate to define function by taking into account not just size, but also the material remains found inside.

The Gargalartepesi settlement provided some evidence of internal features, and building 1 is interesting in this respect, surviving two building phases (10). The construction underwent repair even from its earliest period. Walls, which consisted of a single line of bricks in the northeast and southwest sections, were strengthened by a retaining wall. In the northeast section the hearth was extended to join the walls and by so doing the wall here was destroyed, later to be filled with clay. Inside, the northern wall has a section of very reddish discolouration, including the floor area below. During a period of repair, the retaining wall partially closed off the centre and there are brick remains in this area of the floor. Here also (at 55 cm) were found the remains of a clay vessel 80 cm in diameter. The sides of the vessel were 8-10 cm thick in places and one side was pierced with a hole 15 cm in diameter. The second floor was found 55 cm above the first, and there was yellow clay separating them. In this floor, by the western wall, a crude clay vessel was found (diameter 38 cm, sides 4 cm thick). The hearth is again at the east wall. As indicated, building 1 is a dwelling, with its centre, and a vessel, located in the floor — features retained through both inhabited levels.

Building 12 is also interesting. The floor has been covered repeatedly and painted with dark red paint. In the centre there is a 12-14 cm hole, probably the remains of a central post. The hearth is at the east wall. The many floor coverings, and 2 metres of walling remains, suggest a long period of construction. Taking into account the building's location, in a complex (with a walled courtyard with entrance) that included cylindrical towers, it is possible to ascertain its detached situation. The absence of an entrance in a two-meter stretch of wall is indicative of a special structure. If it were not for the hearth it could have been a storehouse, but its particular features point to a cult construction.

The constructions at Shomutepe are easier to attribute. Typically they are clearly dwellings or non-dwellings, and intermediate forms have not been found. The sole non-dwelling (building 5) has a large hearth 70 cm in diameter, containing ashes up to 10 cm deep (8). But the location of a hearth in the centre of so small a space (only 2 metres in diameter) precludes its use as a dwelling. The other eight constructions (denoted in Roman numerals) were also non-dwelling units. Buildings 1 and 2 did not retain enough material to allow their functions to be determined, but buildings 3, 4, 5, 6, 7, 8, and 9 were clearly dwellings. Their internal layouts were simple — clay-covered floor and walling, with entrance aperture slightly higher than the floor, and hearth located against the wall opposite the entrance. Non-dwelling X (2.1 m in diameter) is of special interest. The entrance is 45 cm wide and level with the floor. On the floor around the entrance were green-coloured stratifications - traces of cattle manure. Taking into account the size of the building and its entrance, this site was intended as a stable for small species of livestock.

The constructions at Toyretepe were not well preserved and only building 22 can be discussed with any certainty. This structure is 3.2 m in diameter and had a clay-covered floor. The 50 cm-wide entrance is located in the northeast section. Inside, and to the right of the entrance, there were three unfired vessels dug into the floor; a similar vessel was found by the east wall. These vessels were clearly moulded into pre-dug holes in the floor. (Such pots — both fired and unfired — are characteristic of the sites investigated.) Buildings 2 and 3 were probably non-dwellings. They contained semicircular partitions, and building 2 appears to have had two of them existing serially.

Of the twelve numbered constructions at Ilanlitepe, only buildings 7 and 11 may be assessed from their internal features (39). The remaining ten numbered and five unnumbered buildings can only be described by their layouts. Building 7 is the largest and has the most interesting form; excavations allowed the interpretation of 60% of it. The shape is ovoid (5 m) and two internal walls divide the dug out area of the construction into two parts. One of these walls has a door aperture 70 cm wide. The floor is covered with a dark-red coat, with some traces of ashes. In the northeast corner there is a brick hearth full of ash; the bricks have reddened and the wall behind has blackened. Two other features were found in the northwest of the premises. The first was a semicircular partition contiguous to the wall, and the second a curious niche that cut through the wall. The entrance to the construction was not found; it was probably in the unexcavated southwest section. Many finds were cleared from the premises — vessels, as well as clay, stone and bone implements. The nature of the layout of building 7, as well as its finds, allow us to fix it as a dwelling of relatively high status. Building 11 has a completely different layout, being trapezoidal in form. The floor of the premises is carefully covered with a clay solution painted in a light red colour. Traces of the same colour were found on the west wall. The premises had an entrance 1 m wide in the southeast wall; the threshold was at floor level. A circular hole (15 cm wide, 20 cm deep) — probably from a door post - was found near the entrance. Outside, a continuation of the walls created a sort of forward section, and there was probably no overlapping. Here there is a small semicircular extension contiguous to the southwest wall of the courtyard. The interior did not reveal any material remains. In the courtyard a horn mattock and a bone needle were found. The absence of hearth and other material features raises doubts over the function of the premises.

Building 8 at Alikemektepesi consists of two spaces and is of interest. The premises are separated by a passage approximately 1 m wide. The main entrance did not survive. One space is a large oval premises, with a round platform (30 cm diameter) near the entrance, raised above a floor (at 13 cm). The clay platform included ceramic fragments and similar platforms have been found in other buildings, and all include ceramic fragments inserted on the upper surfaces. F.R. Mahmudov, the site investigator, considers these to be seats or a form of table for utensils (2, p.57), but the protruding fragments detract from this theory somewhat. Inside the premises there were various finds, including ten different utensils, clay artifacts, and a bone mattock. The floor (about 11 sq. m) showed remains of matting. By the northern wall there are the remains of an open hearth. The second space is about 5.5 sq. m and contained the remains of various household goods, indicating that this was a non-dwelling area.

Another common feature of this settlement is the presence of cylindrical vessels dug into the floor. One such vessel reached 1.4 m in height and 1 m in diameter (2, p.61). In the corners and along the walls of building 94, similar vessels were found — some up to 70 cm in height. Most likely these contained grain and their presence in the settlement may explain the absence of grain pits (in the Eneolithic period) (2. p.62). Building 40 retained interior elements relating to a secondary construction phase (level 2.1 m). The floor of the premises was covered many times — the thickness of the coat reaching 5-6 cm (3, p.10). In the centre there were the remains of a hearth with a diameter of approximately 1 m. In the southwest corner there were the remains of a sunken clay vessel, 45 cm in diameter, 22 cm high, and with walls 4 cm thick.

At Kultepe 1, at a level of 21.4 m, the earliest hearth of the settlement was revealed. It was probably rectangular in form, and a section remained of its walls, 30 cm wide. At its centre was an oval construction with axes 1 m x 0.8 m, and a remaining height of 80 cm. The walls of the hearth were formed of stones mortared with clay. The oval pit had a large axis of about 1 m and a depth 90 cm: it was filled with ashes (18, p.25-26). Other excavations revealed a clay furnace of oval form, with axes 1 m x 0.55 m and a retained height of 30 cm, and wall thickness of 5-6 cm (18, p.26). The furnace relates to a construction, the floor of which remains with remnants of matting. Kultepe 1, therefore, shows us that certain interior features, such as hearths and furnaces, were present even in the lowest layers and were relatively advanced. Conditions on site prevented the investigation of other features.

In the Early Bronze Age layer of Kultepe 1, building 33 (at 13 m) is of particular interest. It is constructed of crude brick and has a diameter of 8.35 m (18, p.83). The space is divided into two unequal parts by a brick wall and the floors are covered with a layer of clay on which were found ashes and by pieces of coal. In the northeast section of the smaller part there were plentiful remains of burnt grain, indicating that this part was probably a food storage area.

Building 15/20 consists of two spaces with a diameter of 5.2 m: its walls were 48-50 cm thick. There was also a rectangular extension (18, p.91). The main area is divided into two unequal parts by a brick wall 18 cm thick. Half way along the wall there is an opening 90 cm wide. The entrance to the premises is 110 cm wide and located in the northeast section of the smaller part. The rectangular extension adjoins the unit from the south. Here there is 70 cm-wide entrance into the larger half of the circular premises. In the centre of the circular space were the remains of a hearth dug into the floor around which was a layer of ashes. At the southwest part of the floor there was a layer of fine gravel. The floor of the rectangular extension was covered with a layer of ashes. The overall complex must represent a dwelling comprising three distinct spaces — a smaller front space, the main dwelling area with hearth and cooking vessel, and the food storage area.

Building 1/2 consists of a main circular space joined at the southeast by a rectangular extension. Using the scanty remains of the walls, a diameter of 13 m may be estimated for the main circular space. The clay walls, 70 cm thick, were built on a stone base. The walls of the rectangular area were 50 cm thick and made of clay mass (18, p.98). The entrance between the two spaces has not survived. The main entrance to the complex was in the circular section, in the southwest part. It was 1 m wide and the threshold contained a stone for the door post. The floor of the round area was covered by a thick layer of clay. There were the remains of a hearth which contained charcoal fragments. The hearth area was 35 cm deep and 30 cm in diameter; there were four stones around it and a cooking vessel survived next to it. Inside, near the southwest wall of the rectangular construction, there was a platform 30 cm high and approximately 15 cm wide. The floor was covered with clay. Except for its relatively large size, building 1/2 is similar to other constructions of the Early Bronze Age layer. The author of the excavation, O.H. Habibullaev, writes that the size of the building suggests that it might have been a public space (18, p.98).

At Yaniktepe, the walls and the floors were covered with plaster. The walls of one construction retained traces of red paint. The same paint is also found on the floors at Haji Firuz, where some constructions are 4 m x 6.5 m and have dedicated internal storage areas (14, p.138).

Ideological representations of the Eneolithic tribes are so far extremely limited. In Azerbaijan, where there are many tombs in the territory of the settlements and a large number of monuments have been investigated, we have just one cult construction, and only a few isolated facts that shed light on religious attitudes.

Archaeological material from Kur-Araz does allow us to speculate about cults, religious rites, etc. Growth in production not only encouraged the fast and widespread distribution of some innovations in what is thought of as material culture, but it also promoted the development of ideological representations. As well as the earliest agricultural cults, new believes sprang up fostered by the significant changes in economic and social life.

Kultepe 1 has constructions of possible cult significance. In particular there is a multi-roomed construction from the Eneolithic layer. Adjoining it is a large circular space of Early Bronze Age date. The size differs from other constructions on the site, and it is possible that it was used for public purposes, i.e. as a cult building. The author of the excavation expresses doubts as to this interpretation because of the absence of any specific finds (18, p.243). It is curious that these constructions were found in the same location, separated by a layer of about 10 m (18, p.239). Perhaps the location was retained as a cult site over a long period.

Alikemektepesi has a pit-house 22 with a diameter of 3 m and it differs in some features from others on the site. Its walls are covered with a thick layer of clay, on which various patterns have been painted - circles, semicircles, parallel lines, and dots (2, p.59). On the basis of this decoration, the excavation authors consider the construction of some cult significance (33, p.13).

Conclusions

The study of the huge amount of archaeological material available, and its analysis in an architectural context, has shown that a distinctive architectural tradition, with its own characteristic building materials, styles, layouts, and designs, may be traced from earliest times. Research indicates that the most ancient settlements developed rapidly around a central core area. Simultaneously with each construction phase there was a rise in the level of the settlement. In due course settlements that usually began on a flat plane developed into mounds. Similar developments resulted in the formation of large artificial hills or tells, reaching heights of more than 20 m, as at Kultepe 1, and occupying areas of up to 5 hectares, as at Khinitepe.

We have methodically investigated all the cultural layers available, based on archaeological excavations. Detailed study of the monuments concerned has enabled us to comprehend the formation processes of these layers and the detailed stratigraphy of the constructions contained in them.

The most significant innovation to appear from the scientific research is the new technique of construction-layer definition. Special attention was paid to settlement planning and existing theories were reviewed completely. The result is the most accurate picture to date of planning structure, function, and inhabitation.

Archaeological studies since 1976 of those settlements that can be differentiated by their cultural remains, from the Mesolithic in Gobustan, to the medieval in Kharaba-Gilan, have allowed us to trace the various structural phenomena in the formation of all cultural layers. As to the periods under review here, the nature of the cultural remains (Eneolithic and Early Bronze Age phases) investigated by us at Chalagantepe, Leylatepesi, Durnatepe, Keniza, Ana Zaga etc., shows that the accumulated mass of cultural remains at these settlements were laid down sequentially. The complex nature of the cultural layer is expressed by the juxtaposed remains of building materials and non-domestic waste that present significant difficulties for the study of the architecture. This is especially true of the study of settlement planning and its basic elements — the inhabited unit, the inhabited complex, the inhabited group: the dynamics of development that define the structure of the evolution of settlement planning. Some of the difficulties were addressed by analyzing the cultural layer through its component parts. Major components of any cultural layer are represented by certain horizontal planes which define certain concrete 'moments' in the history of the settlement. Based on these particular significant 'moments', it is then possible to make further hypotheses and generalizations. These generalizations help to simplify the study of settlement planning and to allocate structural planning changes within the limits of certain time intervals that cover the most significant changes. Obviously, these generalizations are artificial when applied to the allocated limits of construction layers. At the same time, our generalizations have their own self-imposed laws, such as the impossibility of structural overlap and the stratigraphical conformity arising from the architectural integrity of inhabited complexes. Sites such as the settlements at Toyretepe, Gargalartepesi, Shomutepe, Alikemektepesi, Chalagantepe have today been thoroughly studied using this architectural view point

Analysis of settlement planning has revealed many similarities in the majority of sites. There are two basic settlement construction types — the most common being those with round buildings and associated layout, such as Kultepe 1 (where a very few rectangular constructions were also found), Kultepe 2, Gargalartepesi, Shomutepe, Baba-Dervish, Garakepektepe (bottom layer), Toyretepe, Chalagantepe, Guneshtepe, Alikemektepesi

(3rd-5th layers), Yaniktepe, and Borispoltepe. The other type consists of rectangular buildings and their associated layout, such as at Alikemektepesi (1st-2nd layers), Leylatepesi, Garakepektepe (upper layer), and Ilanlitepe (where both types have been found).

Planning studies have also shown that settlements made up of round-plan buildings have a distinct layout for their domestic complexes (i.e. domestic and non-domestic constructions located around a functioning courtyard). Thus, certain settlements have shown individual planning characteristics. The eight upper layers of Chalagantepe had their courtyards bordered by buildings, whereas at Shomutepe, and in the bottom two layers at Chalagantepe, the courtyards were also protected by an enclosure. The same is also the case at Gargalartepesi, but in an even more original way, where the public complex has an enclosure with its own elaborate entrance.

1.2 million years have passed since the appearance of man in what we now know of as Azerbaijan, and over the millennia a distinct architectural tradition has evolved with its own originality and tradition. From the earliest Palaeolithic stone partitions in the Azikh caves, and proceeding to the Mesolithic and Neolithic structures of Gobustan, this tradition is traced in both the general culture and in the architecture. With the development of economic opportunities and technology, architecture and construction entered a new era of intensive activity that, in turn, resulted in further technological advances.

The comparative analysis of monuments from all the historical phases of Azerbaijan and Eurasia shows surprising stability and the traditional local character of the material culture, including architecture — from the Mesolithic stonework of Gobustan to that of the recent past in Baku and Absheron.

In all its historical phases, the development of architecture in Azerbaijan occupied a leading role. The medieval school of architecture in Tebriz — the capital of the Sefevi region — influenced design and construction from the Alps to India and China, Eurasia to Northern Africa. This did not happen by chance: it was the result of centuries of deep-rooted tradition stretching back to the pre-historical monuments, including the extraordinary sites that form the basis of this particular research.

Bibliography /Azeri

Исмајылов Г. С. Хантепе енеолит абидяси вя онун Азярбайъанын щямдювр абидяляри арасында йери. Даш дюврц вя Азярбайъанда енеолит. Бакы, 1984.
Ismayilov G. S. Khantepe eneolit abidesi ve onun Azerbaijanin hemdevr abideleri arasinda yeri. Dash devru ve Azerbaijanda eneolit. Baki, 1984.

Мащмудов Ф. Р. Яликюмяк тяпясиндя археоложи газынтыларын илкин йекунлары. Даш дюврц вя Азярбайъанда енеолит. Бакы, 1984. Mahmudov F. R. Alikemek tepesinde arkheoloji gazintilarin ilkin yekunlari. Dash devru ve Azerbaijanda eneolit. Baki, 1984.

Мащмудов Ф. Р., Няриманов И. Щ. Муьан археоложи дястясинин 1975-ъи ил тядгигатларынын щесабаты. Азярбайъан Елмляр Академийасы Тарих Институтунун архиви. № Щ-159.
Mahmudov F. R., Narimanov I. H. Mugan arkheoloji destesinin 1975 il tedgigatlarinin hesabati. Azerbaijan Elmler Akademiyasi Tarikh Institutunun arkhivi. No. Sh-159.

Мащмудов Ф. Р., Няриманов И. Щ. Муьан археоложи дястясинин 1977-ъи ил тядгигатларынын щесабаты. Азярбайъан Елмляр Академийасы Тарих Институтунун архиви. № Щ-204.
Mahmudov F. R., Narimanov I. H. Mugan arkheoloji destesinin 1977 il tedgigatlarinin hesabati. Azerbaijan Elmler Akademiyasi Tarikh Institutunun arkhivi. No. Sh-204.

Мащмудов Ф. Р., Няриманов И. Щ. Муьан археоложи дястясинин 1976-ъи ил тядгигатларынын щесабаты. Азярбайъан Елмляр Академийасы Тарих Институтунун архиви. № Щ-201.
Mahmudov F. R., Narimanov I. H. Mugan arkheoloji destesinin 1976 il tedgigatlarinin hesabati. Azerbaijan Elmler Akademiyasi Tarikh Institutunun arkhivi. No. Sh-201.

Мурадова Ф.М. Гобустан тунъ дюврцндя. Бакы, 1979.
Muradova F. M. Gobustan tunj devrinde. Baki, 1979.

Няриманов И. Щ. Газах археоложи експедисийасынын щесабаты. Азярбайъан Елмляр Академийасы Тарих Институтунун архиви. № 5979.
Narimanov I. H. Gazakh arkheoloji ekspedisiyasinin hesabati. Azerbaijan Elmler Akademiyasi Tarikh Institutunun arkhivi. No. 5979.

Няриманов И. Щ. 1963-ъц илдя Газах археоложи експедисийасынын щесабаты. Азярбайъан Елмляр Академийасы Тарих Институтунун архиви. № 5548.
Narimanov I. H. 1963 ilde Gazakh arkheoloji ekspedisiyasinin hesabati. Azerbaijan Elmler Akademiyasi Tarikh Institutunun arkhivi. No. 5548.

Няриманов И. Щ., Мащмудов Ф. Р. 1972-ъи илдя Эянъя-Газах археоложи дястясинин апардыьы чюл-тядгигат ишляринин щесабаты. Азярбайъан Елмляр Академийасы Тарих Институтунун архиви. № 7498, щ-75. Narimanov I. H., Mahmudov F. R. 1972 ilde Genje-Gazakh arkheoloji destesinin apardigi choltedgigat ishlerinin hesabati. Azerbaijan Elmler Akademiyasi Tarikh Institutunun arkhivi. No. 7498, sh-75.

Няриманов И. Щ., Мащмудов Ф. Р. 1971-ъи илдя Гарьалар тяпяси вя Яликюмяк тяпясиндя апарылмыш газынтыларын щесабаты. Азярбайъан Елмляр Академийасы

Тарих Институтунун архиви. Narimanov I. H., Mahmudov F. R. 1971 ilde Gargalar tepesi ve Alikemek tepesinde aparilmish gazintilarin hesabati. Azerbaijan Elmler Akademiyasi Tarikh Institutunun arkhivi.

Щябибуллайев О. Щ. Кцлтяпядя археоложи газынтылар. Бакы, 1959. Habibullayev O. H. Kultepede arkheoloji gazintilar. Baki, 1959.

English

Burton-Brown T. Excavations in Azerbaijan. 1948, London, 1951.

Burney C. A. Circular Buildings Found at Yanik-Tepe in North-West Iran. Antiquity. Cambridge, 1961, XXXV, No 939.

Burney C. A. Excavations at Yanik-Tepe. North-West Iran. Iraq, v. XXIII, No 2, 1961.

Clark G., Piggot S. Prehistoric societies. London, Hutchinson.

Lloyd S., Safar F. Tell Hassuna. Excavations by the Iraq Government Directorate General of Antiquities in 1943 and 1944, JNES, 1945, October, v. IV, No 4.

Merpert N., Munchaev R. Early agricultural Settlements in the Sinjar Plain. Northern Iraq. Iraq, 1973, v. XXXV, No 2.

Russian

Абибуллаев О. А. Энеолит и бронза на территории Нахичеванской АССР. Баку, 1982.
Abibullaev O. A. Eneolit i bronza na territorii Nakhichevanskoy ASSR. Baku, 1982.

Азимов М. С. Структура планировки энеолитического поселения Чалагантепе. Всесоюзная археологическая конференция «Достижения Советской археологии в XI пятилетке». Тезисы докладов. Баку, 1985.
Azimov M. S. Struktura planirovki eneoliticheskogo poseleniya Chalagantepe. Vsesoyuznaya arkheologicheskaya konferentsiya "Dostijeniya Sovetskoy arkheologii v XI pyatiletke". Tezisi dokladov. Baku, 1985.

Азимов М. С. К вопросу определения структуры планировки древних поселений. Доклады Академии Наук Азербайджанской ССР. т. XLI, № 5, 1985.
Azimov M. S. K voprosu opredeleniya strukturi planirovki drevnikh poseleniy. Dokladi Akademii Nauk Azerbaidjanskoy SSR. Tom XLI, No. 5, 1985.

Азимов М. С. О древней архитектуре Гобустана и её связях с архитектурой Ширвана. Доклады Академии Наук Азербайджанской ССР. т. XLI, № 7, 1985.
Azimov M. S. O drevnei arkhitekture Gobustana i eyo svyazyakh s arkhitekturoy Shirvana. Dokladi Akademii Nauk Azerbaidjanskoy SSR. Tom XLI, No. 7, 1985.

Алиев В. Кюльтепе II - ранний город Азербайджана. Археологические и этнографические изыскания в Азербайджане (1973 г.). Баку, 1974.

Aliev V. Kyultepe II - ranniy gorod Azerbaidjana. Arkheologicheskie i etnograficheskie iziskaniya v Azerbaidjane (1973). Baku, 1974.

Амирджанов Ю. К. Послойная реконструкция строительных сооружений древнего поселения Кюльтепе на территории Нахичеванской АССР. Тезисы докладов на II Республиканской конференции «Проблемы архитектуры и градостроительства». Баку, 1986.
Amirdjanov. Y. K. Posloynaya rekonstruktsiya stroitelnikh soorujeniy drevnego poseleniya Kyultepe na territorii Nakhichevanskoy ASSR. Tezisi dokladov na II Respublikanskoy konferentsii "Problemi arkhitekturi i gradostroitelstva". Baku, 1986.

Ахундов Д. А. Палео-архитектоническая основа генезиса древних жилых и ритуальных сооружений. Учёные записки Азербайджанского Политехнического Института. Серия X, № 1/18, Баку.
Akhundov D. A. Paleo-arkhitektonicheskaya osnova genezisa drevnikh jilikh i ritualnikh soorujeniy. Uchyonie zapiski Azerbaidjanskogo Politekhnicheskogo Instituta. Seriya X, No. 1/18, Baku.

Гаджиев М. Г. Раскопки поселения раннебронзовой эпохи в горном Дагестане. Археологические открытия в СССР, Москва, 1970.
Gadjiev M. G. Raskopki poseleniya rannebronzovoy epokhi v gornom Dagestane. Arkheologicheskie otkritiya v SSSR, Moscow, 1970.

Гусейнов М. М. Палеолит Азербайджана. Каменный век и энеолит в Азербайджане. Баку, 1984.
Guseynov M. M. Paleolit Azerbaidjana. Kamenniy vek i eneolit v Azerbaidjane. Baku, 1984.

Гусейнов М. М. Ранние стадии заселения человека в пещере Азых. Учёные записки Азербайджанского Государственного Университета. № 4, 1979, Серия истории и философии.
Guseynov M. M. Rannie stadii zaseleniya cheloveka v peshere Azikh. Uchyonie zapiski Azerbaidjanskogo Gosudarstvennogo Universiteta. No. 4, 1979, Seriya istorii i filosofii.

Джавахишвили А. И. Строительное дело и архитектура поселений Южного Кавказа V-III тыс. до н.э. Тбилиси, 1973.
Djavakhishvili A. I. Stroitelnoe delo i arkhitektura poseleniy Yujnogo Kavkaza V-III millennia BC. Tbilisi, 1973.

Исмаилов Г. С. Археологическое исследование древнего поселения Баба-Дервиш. Баку, 1977.
Ismailov G. S. Arkheologicheskoe issledovanie drevnego poseleniya Baba-Dervish. Baku, 1977.

Исмаилов Г. С. Раннебронзовая культура Азербайджана. Автореферат докторской диссертации. Тбилиси, 1983.
Ismailov G. S. Rannebronzovaya kultura Azerbaidjana. Avtoreferat doktorskoy dissertatsii. Tbilisi, 1983.

Кигурадзе Т., Дилбарян М. Новые данные о принципах планировки раннеземледельческих поселений Южного Кавказа. IV Международный симпозиум по грузинскому искусству. Тбилиси, 1983.
Kiguradze T., Dilbaryan M. Novie dannie o printsipakh planirovki rannezemledelcheskikh poseleniy Yujnogo Kavkaza. VI Mejdunarodniy simpozium po gruzinskomu iskusstvu. Tbilisi, 1983.

Киквидзе Я. А. Орошение в древней Грузии. Тбилиси, 1963.
Kikvidze Ya. A. Oroshenie v drevney Gruzii. Tbilisi, 1963.

Махмудов Ф. Р., Нариманов И. Г. Раскопки холма Аликемектепеси. Археологические и этнографические изыскания в Азербайджане (1973 г.). Баку, 1974.
Makhmudov F. R., Narimanov I. G. Raskopki kholma Alikemektepesi. Arkheologicheskie i etnograficheskie iziskaniya v Azerbaidjane (1973). Baku, 1974.

Мелларт Дж. Древнейшие цивилизации Ближнего Востока. Москва, 1982.
Mellart J. Drevneyshie tsivilizatsii Blijnego Vostoka. Moscow, 1982.

Мунчаев Р. М., Мерперт Н. Я. Раннеземледельческие поселения северной Месопотамии. Москва, 1981.
Munchaev R. M., Merpert N. Ya. Rannezemledelcheskie poseleniya severnoy Mesopotamii. Moscow, 1981.

Нариманов И. Г. Археологические исследования Шомутепе в 1963 г. Археологические исследования в Азербайджане. Баку, 1965.
Narimanov I. G. Arkheologicheskie issledovaniya Shomutepe v 1963. Arkheologicheskie issledovaniya v Azerbaidjane. Baku, 1965.

Нариманов И. Г. Культура древнейшего земледельческо-скотоводческого населения Азербайджана. Баку, 1987.
Narimanov I. G. Kultura drevneyshego zemledelchesko-skotovodcheskogo naseleniya Azerbaidjana. Baku, 1987.

Нариманов И. Г. Отчет археологических раскопок на энеолитических поселениях Иланлытепе Агдамского района и Рустепеси Шамхорского района в 1967 г. Архив Института Истории Академии Наук Азербайджанской ССР. № 7498.
Narimanov I. G. Otchet arkheologicheskikh raskopok na eneoliticheskikh poseleniyakh Ilanlitepe Agdamskogo rayona i Rustepesi Shamkhorskogo rayona v 1967. Arkhiv Instituta Istorii Akademii Nauk Azerbaidjanskoy SSR. No. 7498.

Нариманов И. Г., Махмудов Ф. Р. Энеолитические памятники Мугани. Известия Академии Наук Азербайджанской ССР. № 2, 1968.
Narimanov I. G., Makhmudov F. R. Eneoliticheskie pamyatniki Mugani. Izvestiya Akademii Nauk Azerbaidjanskoy SSR. No. 2, 1968.

Нариманов И. Г. Отчет археологических раскопок на холме Иланлытепе в 1968 году. Архив Института Истории Академии Наук Азербайджанской ССР.
Narimanov I. G. Otchet arkheologicheskikh raskopok na kholme Ilanlitepe v 1968 godu. Arkhiv Instituta Istorii Akademii Nauk Azerbaidjanskoy SSR.

Пиотровский Б. Б. Поселения медного века в Армении. Советская археология, т. XI, 1949.
Piotrovskiy B. B. Poseleniya mednogo veka v Armenii. Sovetskaya arkheologiya, Tom XI, 1949.

Пиотровский Б. Б. Археология Закавказья. Ленинград, 1949.
Piotrovskiy B. B. Arkheologiya Zakavkazya. Leningrad, 1949.

Рустамов Дж. Н., Мурадова Ф. Н. Раскопки на стоянке Кяниза в Гобустане. Археологические открытия в СССР, Москва, 1975.
Rustamov Dj. N., Muradova F. N. Raskopki na stoyanke Kyaniza v Gobustane. Arkheologicheskie otkritiya v SSSR, Moscow, 1975.

Сарианиди В. И., Кошаленко Г. А. За барханами - прошлое. Москва, 1966.
Sarianidi V. I, Koshalenko G. A. Za barkhanami - proshloe. Moscow, 1966.

Ханзадян Э.В. Энеолитическое поселение близ Кировакана. Советская археология, № 1, 1963.
Khanzadyan E. V. Eneoliticheskoe poselenie bliz Kirovakana. Sovetskaya arkheologiya, No. 1, 1963.

Энеолит СССР, Москва, 1982.
Eneolit SSSR, Moscow, 1982.

Illustrations

Fig. 1. The author

Fig. 2. The author on site in Gobustan

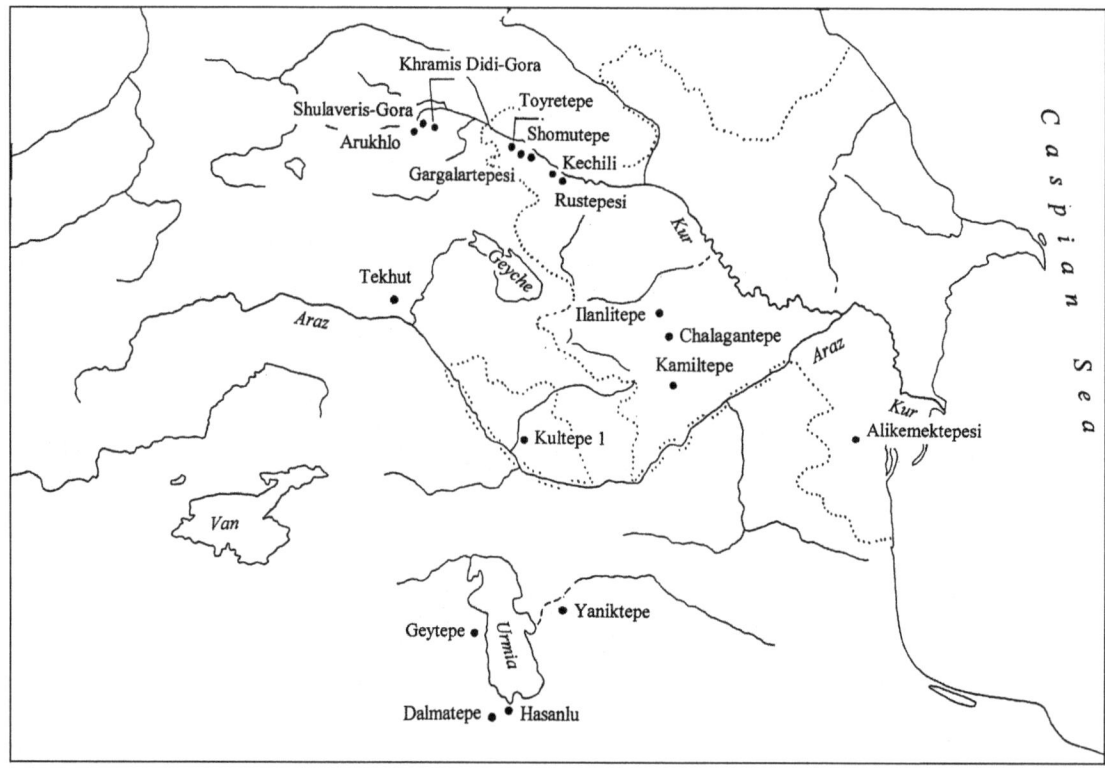

Fig. 3. Distribution map of monuments studied

Fig. 4. Chalagantepe. General view of southern section of the excavation site

Fig. 5. Chalagantepe. General view of northern section of the excavation site

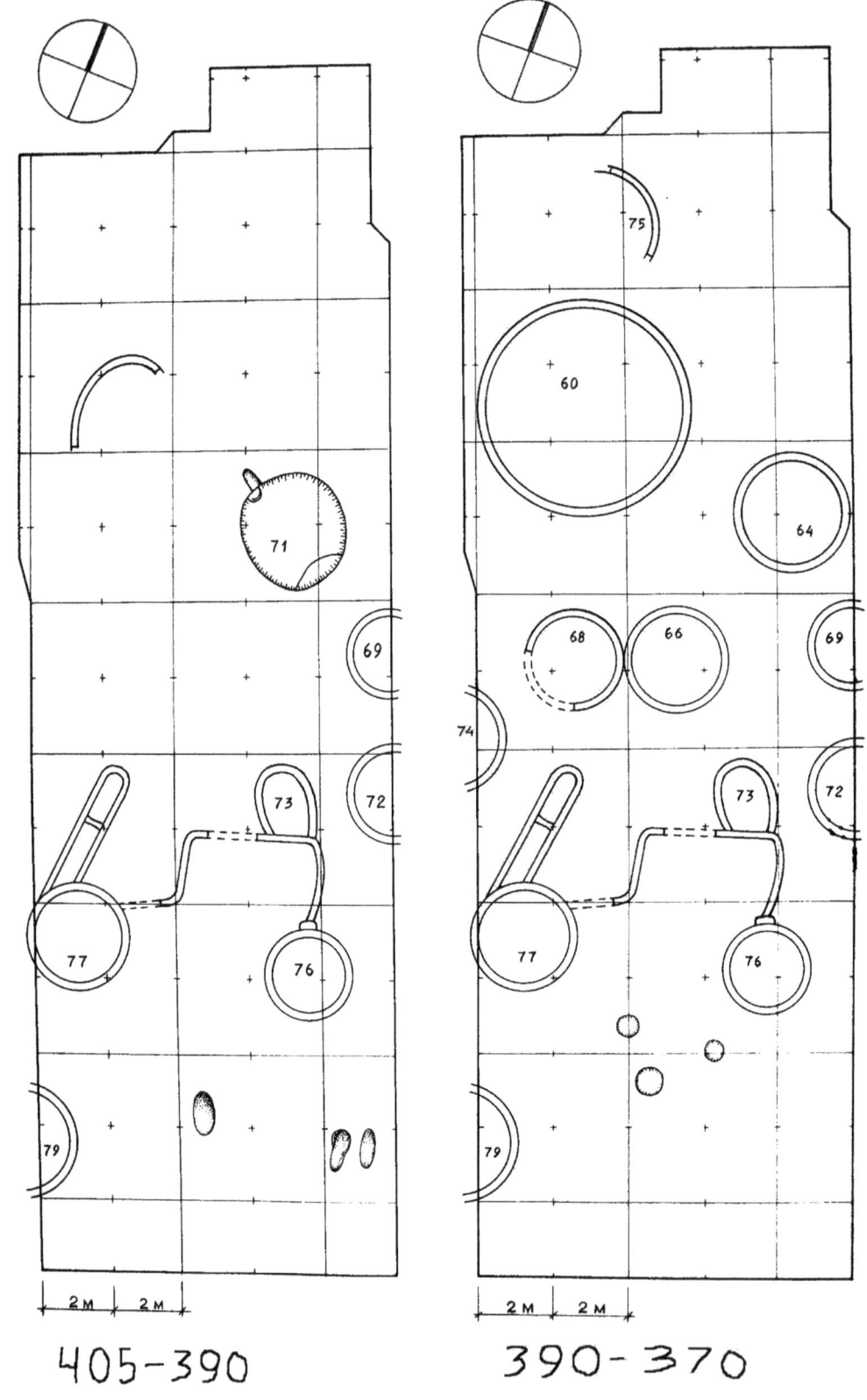

*Fig 6. Chalagantepe.
Plan of level 405-390 cm*

*Fig. 7. Chalagantepe.
Plan of level 390-370 cm*

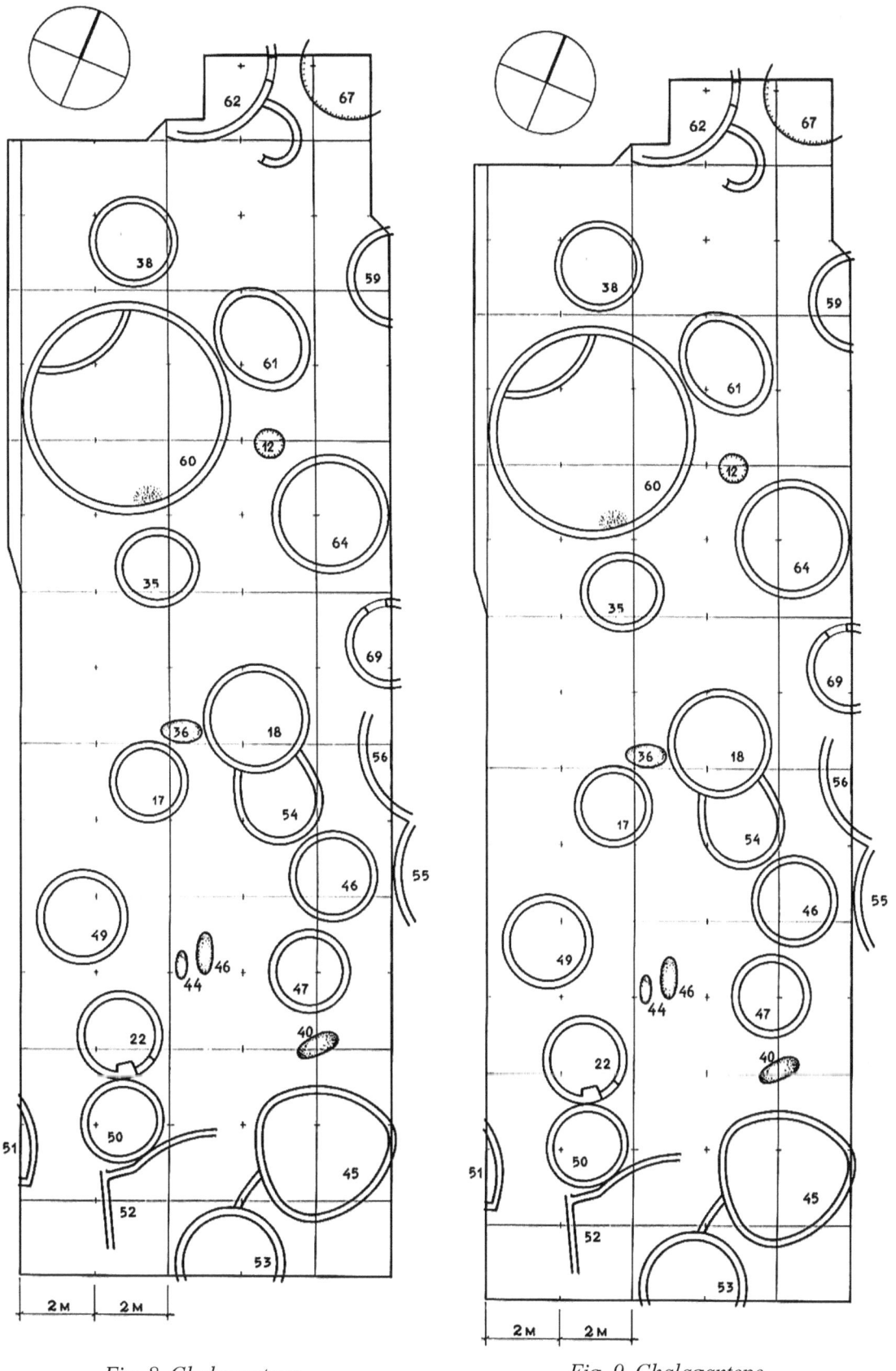

Fig. 8. Chalagantepe. Plan of level 370-350 cm

Fig. 9. Chalagantepe. Plan of level 350-325 cm

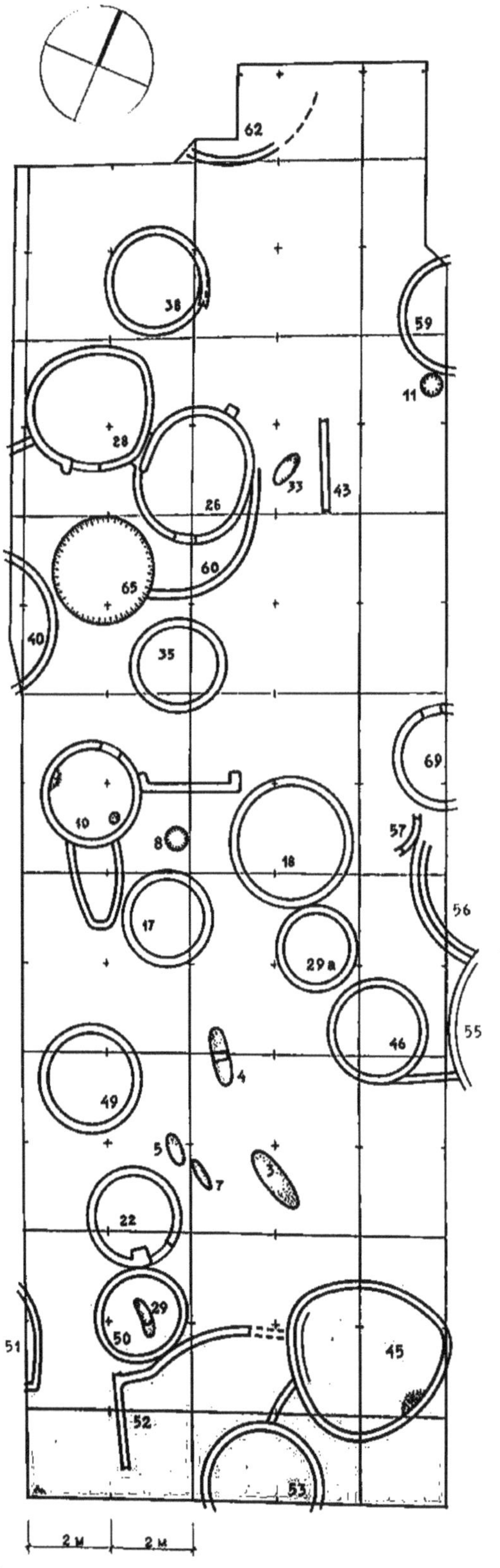

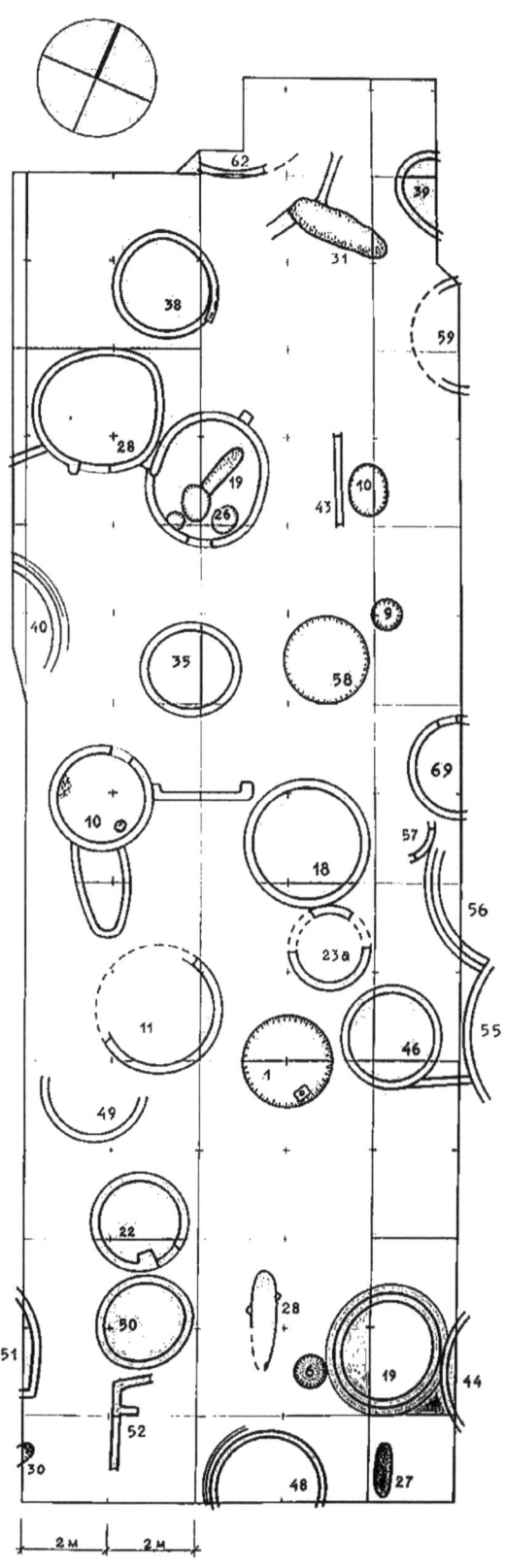

Fig. 10. Chalagantepe.
Plan of level 325-305 cm

Fig. 11. Chalagantepe.
Plan of level 305-290 cm

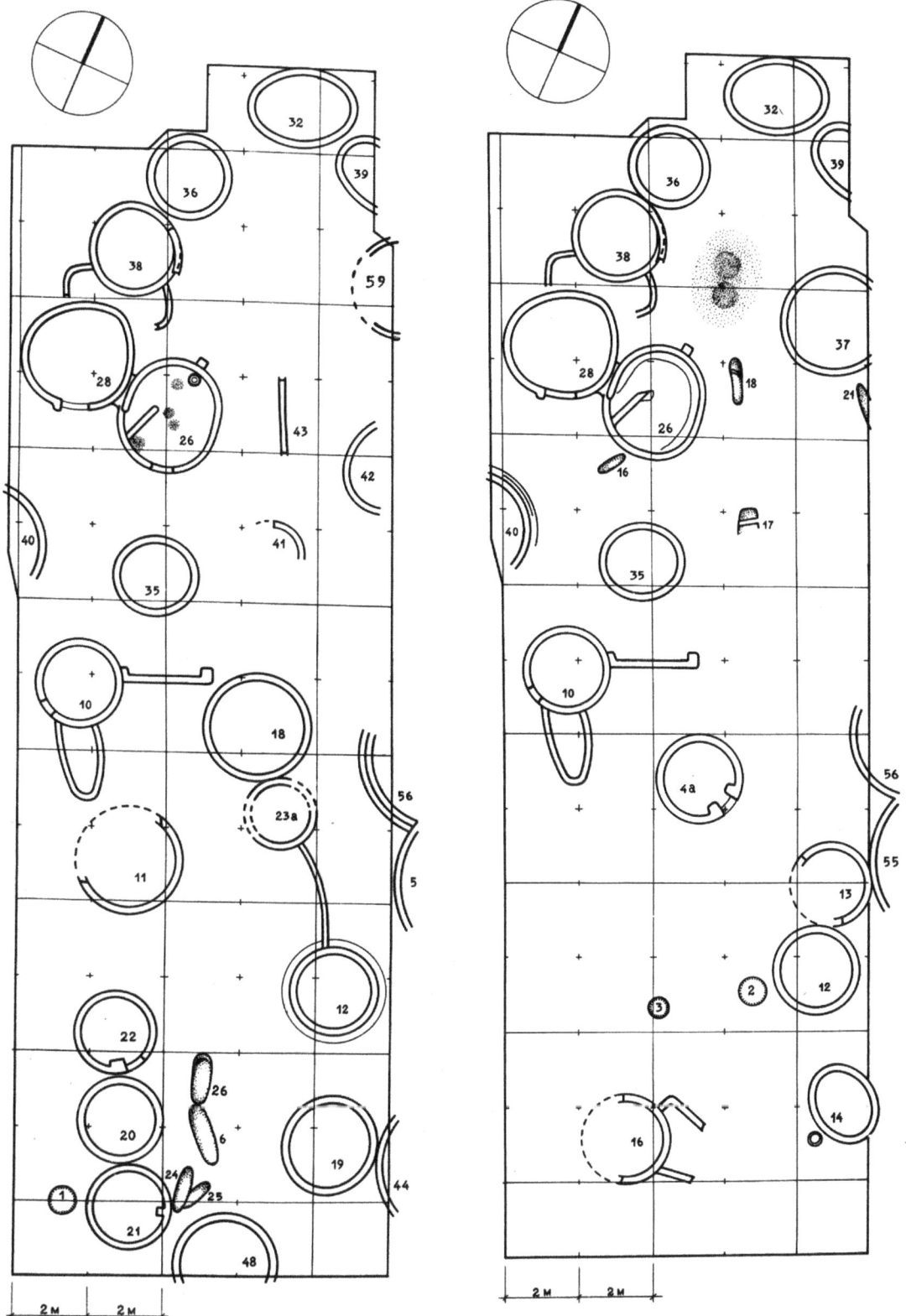

Fig. 12. Chalagantepe.
Plan of level 290-275 cm

Fig. 13. Chalagantepe.
Plan of level 275-255 cm

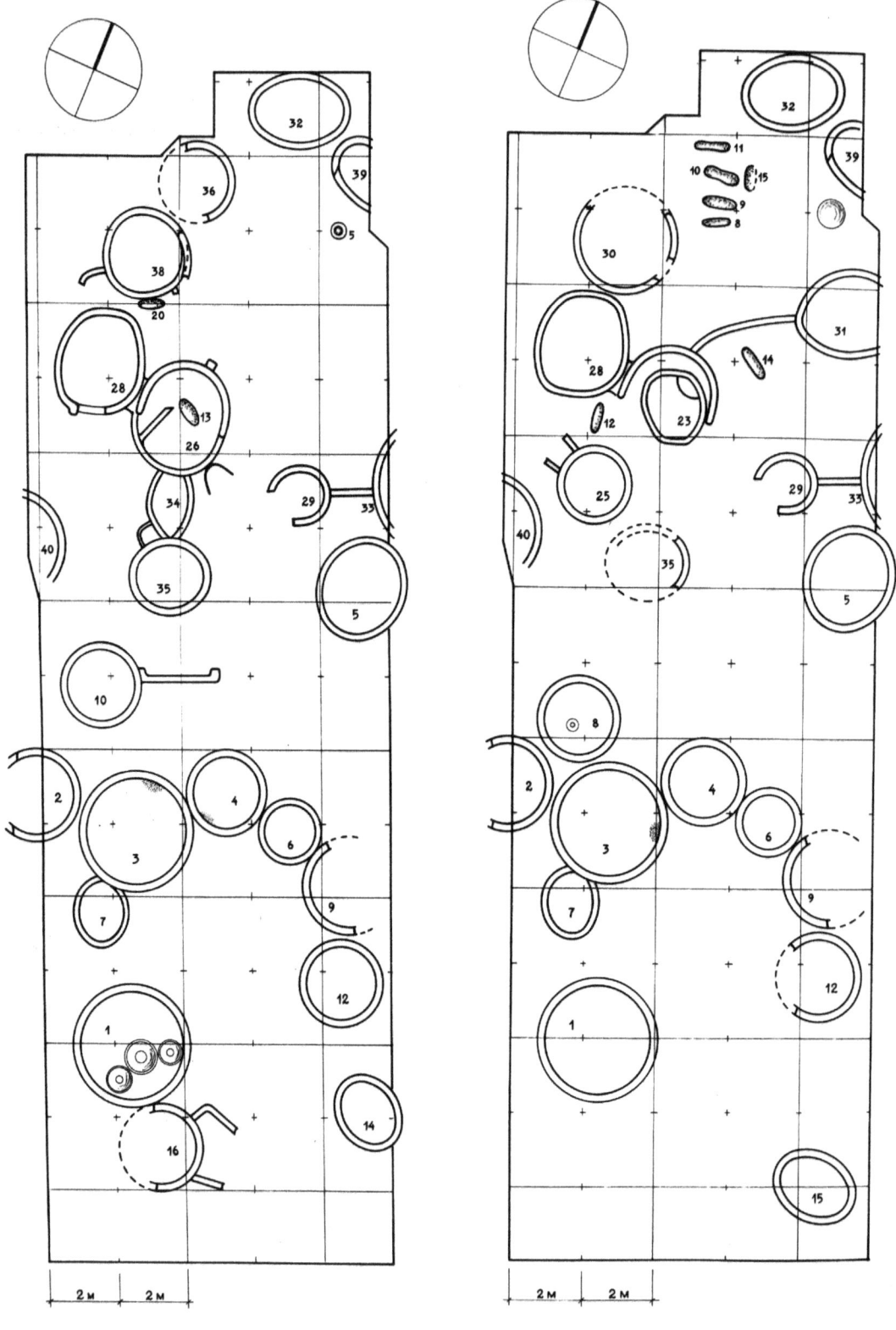

*Fig. 14. Chalagantepe.
Plan of level 255-230 cm*

*Fig. 15. Chalagantepe.
Plan of level 230-208 cm*

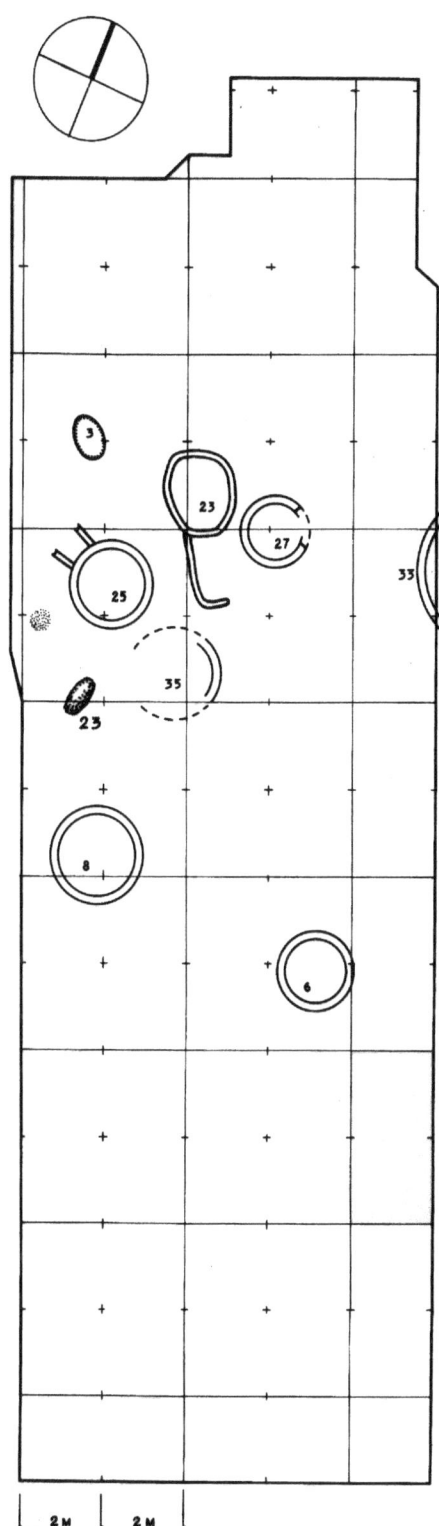

Fig. 16. Chalagantepe.
Plan of level 208-190 cm

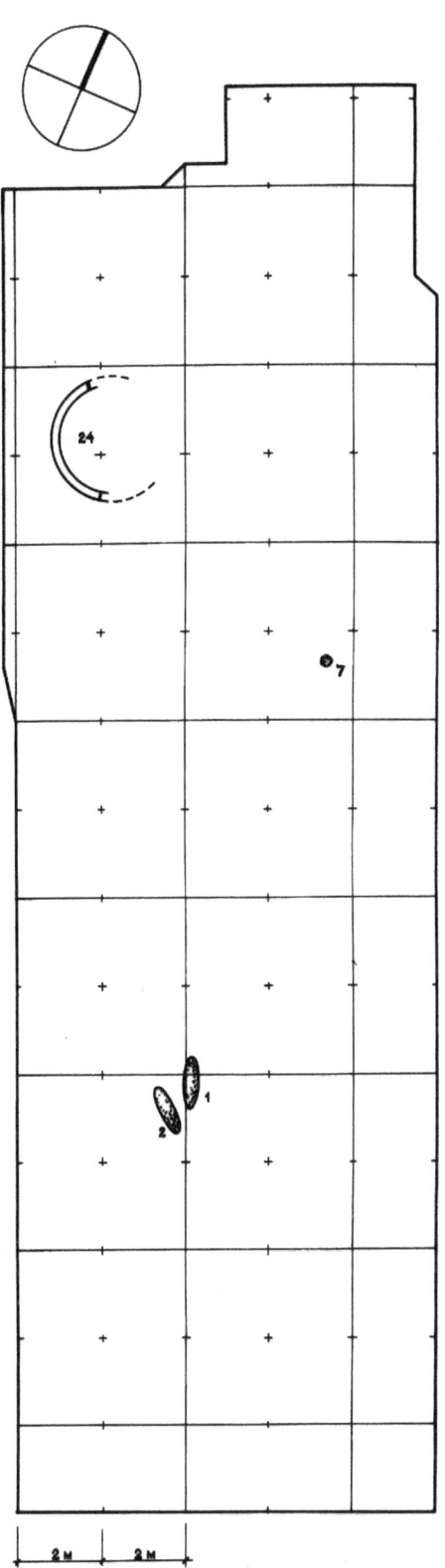

Fig. 17. Chalagantepe.
Plan of level above 190 cm

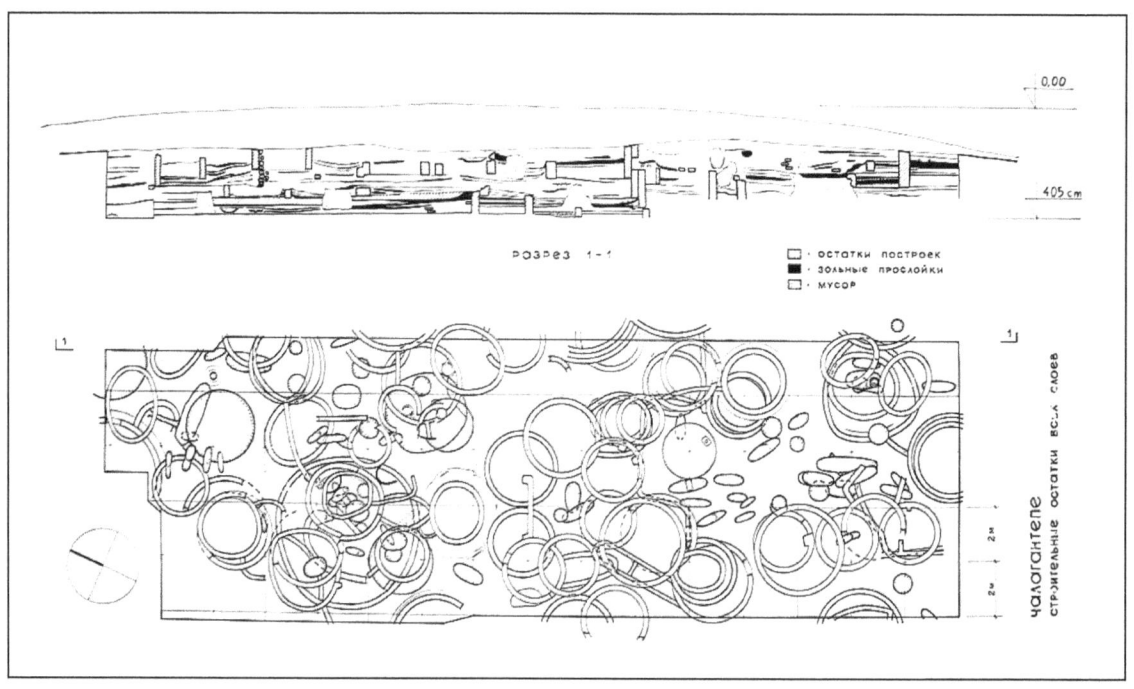

Fig. 18. Chalagantepe. Consolidated plan of all levels (cut on an axis 1-1)

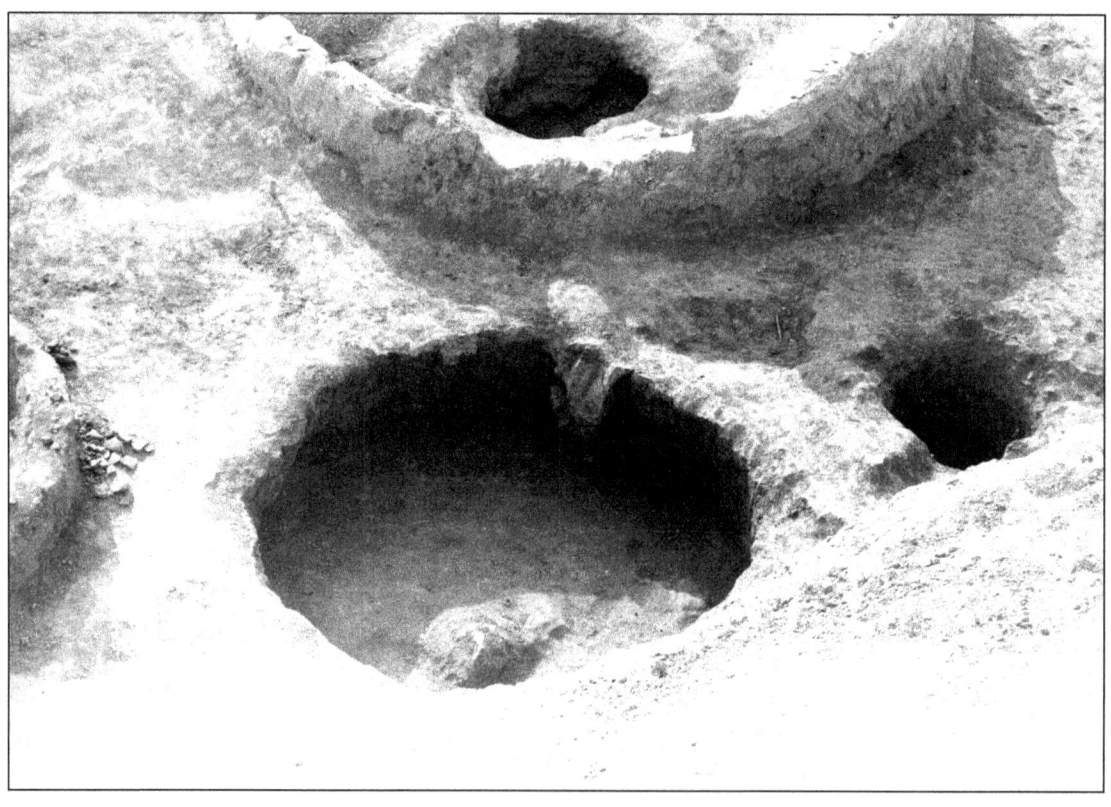

Fig. 19. Chalagantepe. Pit-house dwelling 71

Fig. 20. Chalagantepe. Reconstruction of level 255-230 cm

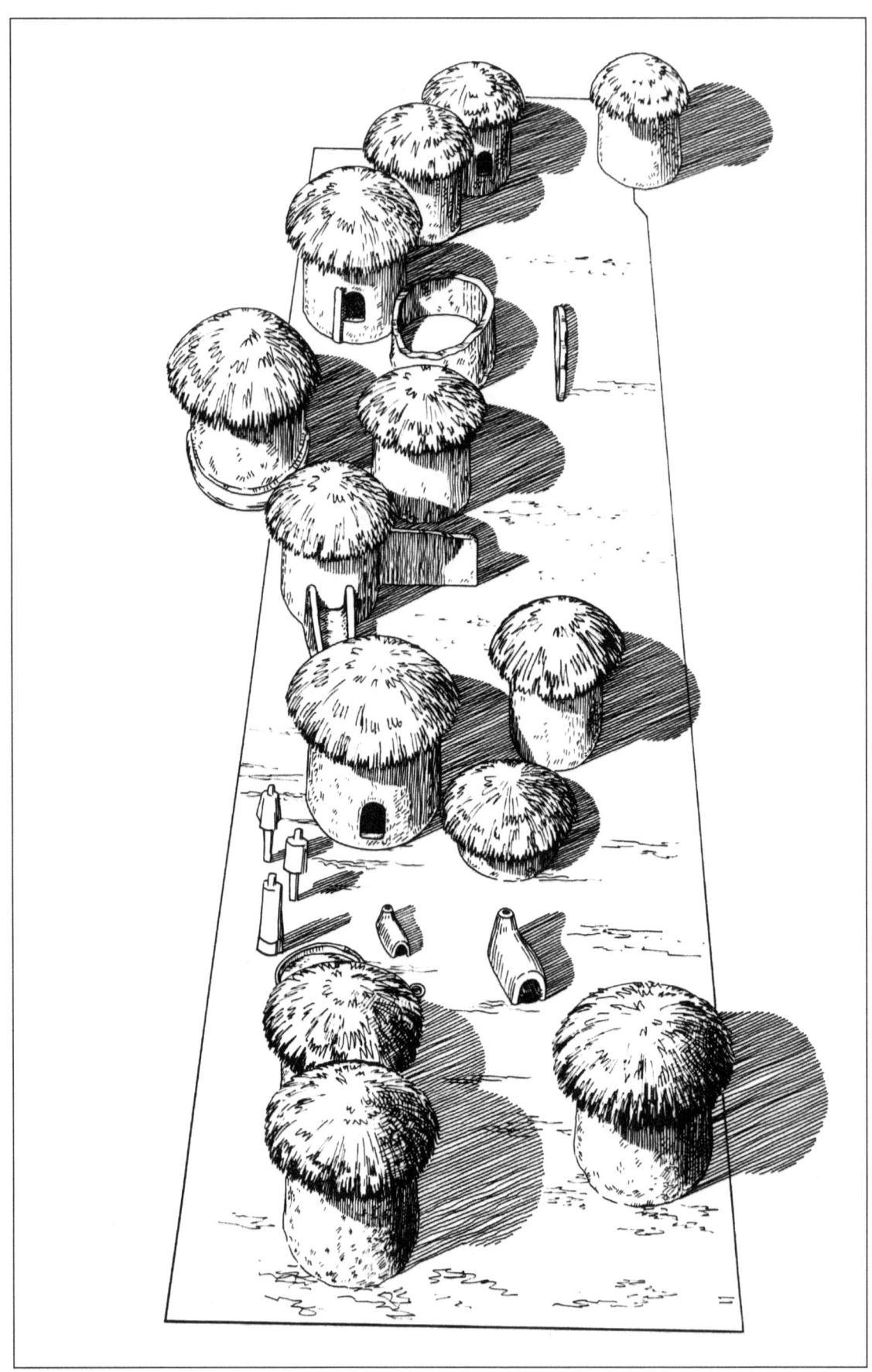

Fig. 21. Chalagantepe. Reconstruction of level 290-275 cm

Fig. 22. Chalagantepe. Building 26

Fig. 23. Chalagantepe. Building 26

Fig. 24. Chalagantepe. "Plano-convex brick" in wall masonry

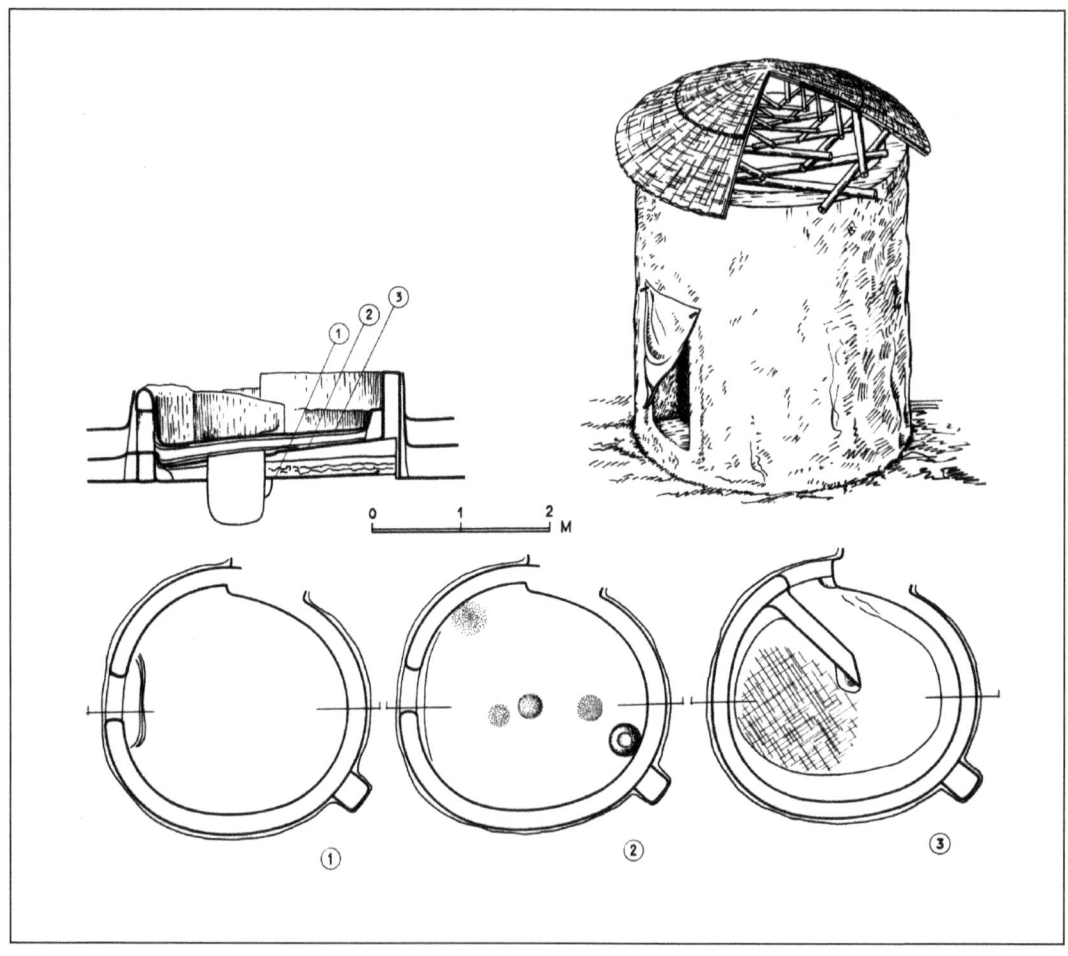

Fig. 25. Chalagantepe. Building 26. Plan of three levels of dwellings, cut and reconstruction

Fig. 26. Chalagantepe. Furnace 31

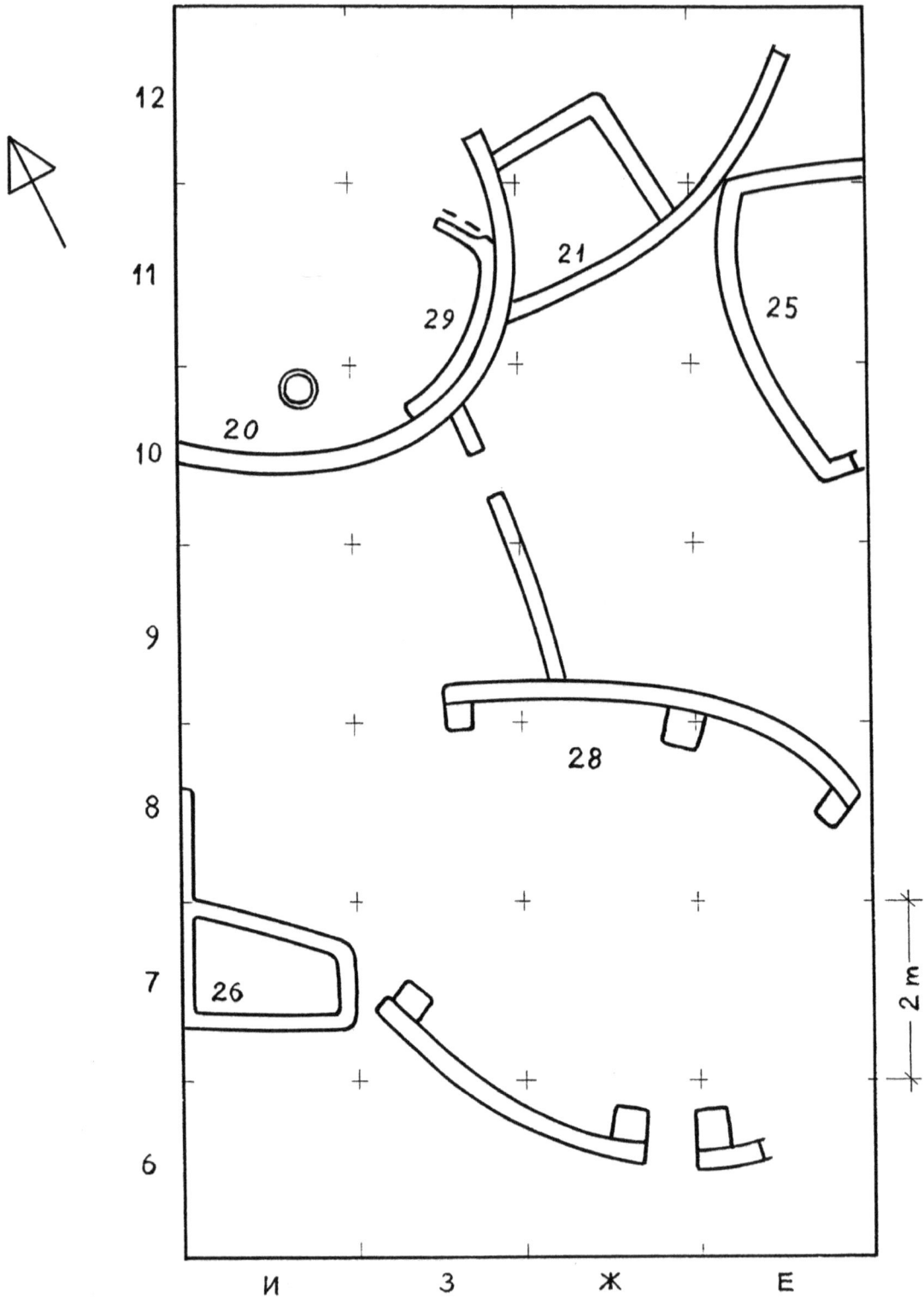

Fig. 27. Alikemektepesi. Plan of construction layer at level 480-380 cm

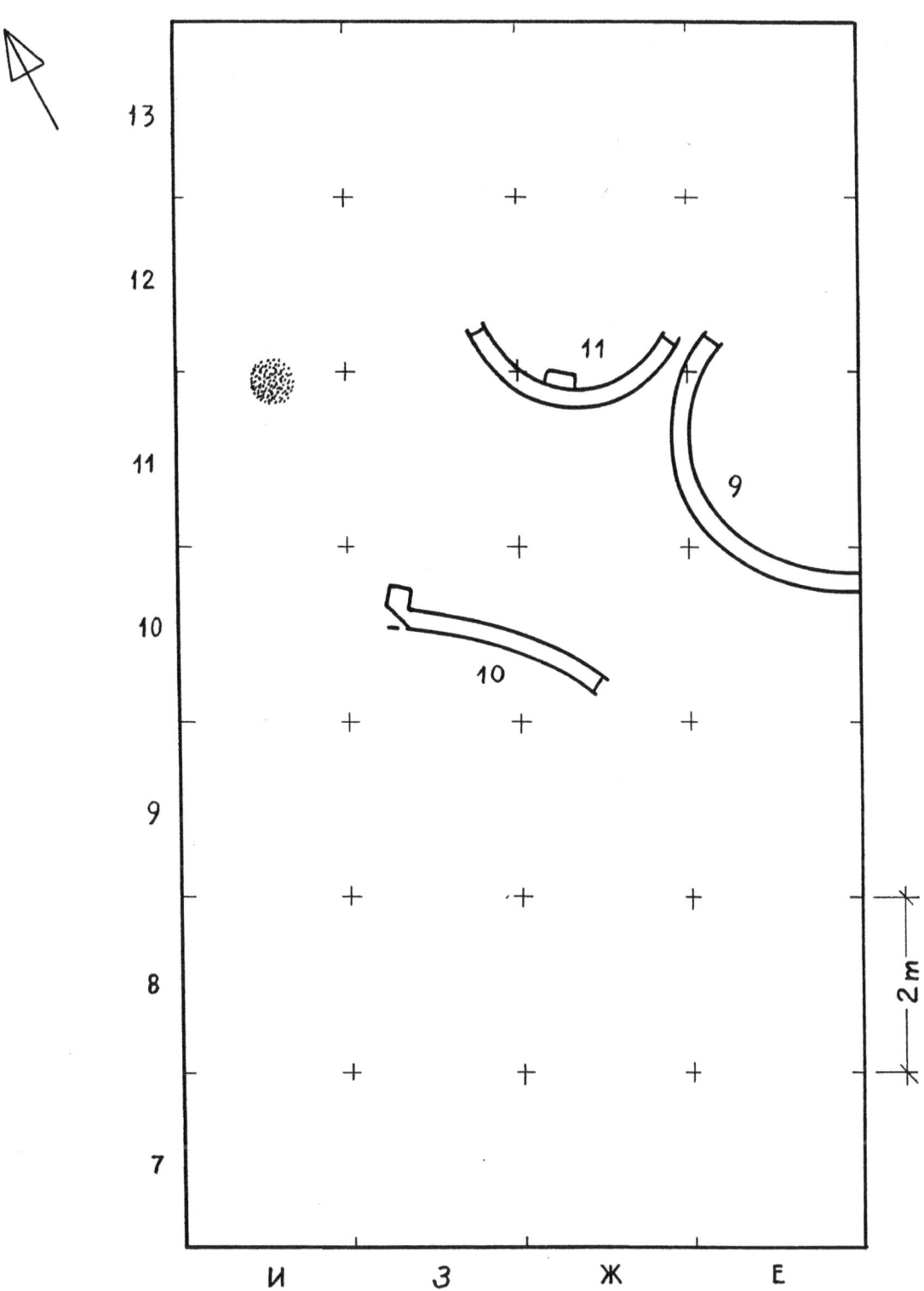

Fig. 28. Alikemektepesi. Plan of construction layer at level 380-280 cm

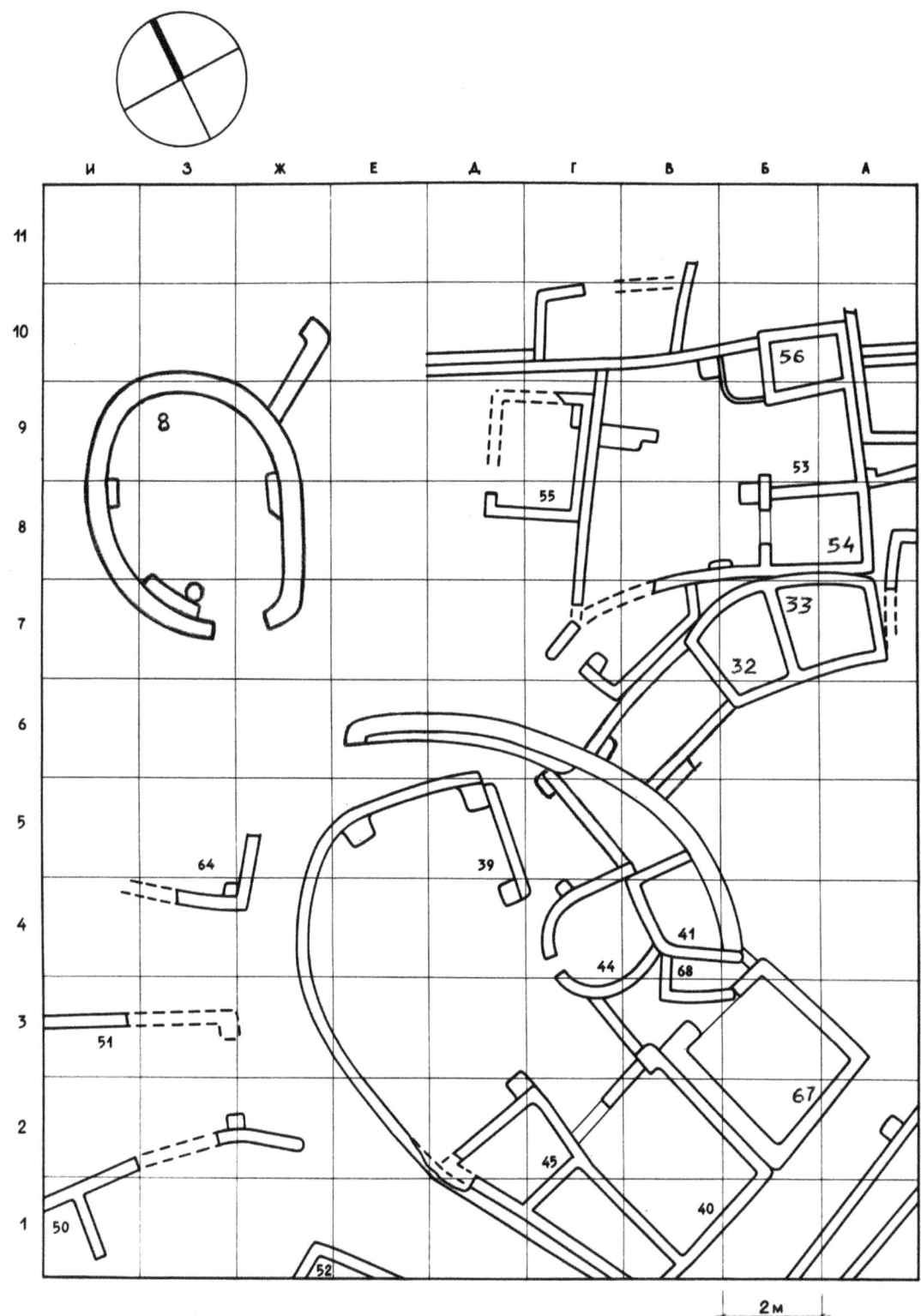

Fig. 29. Alikemektepesi. Plan of construction layer at level 310-210 cm

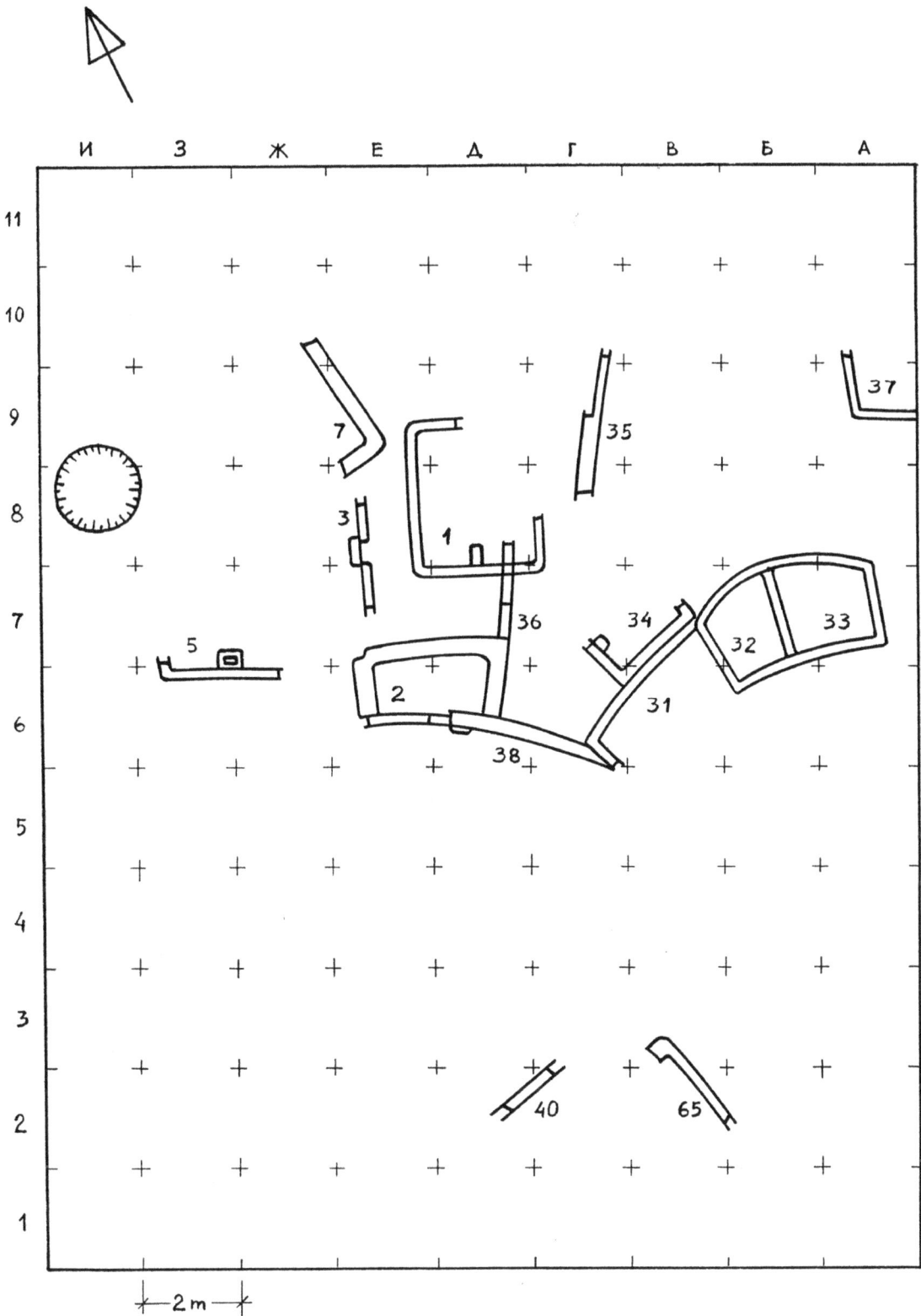

Fig. 30. Alikemektepesi. Plan of construction layer at level 215-130 cm

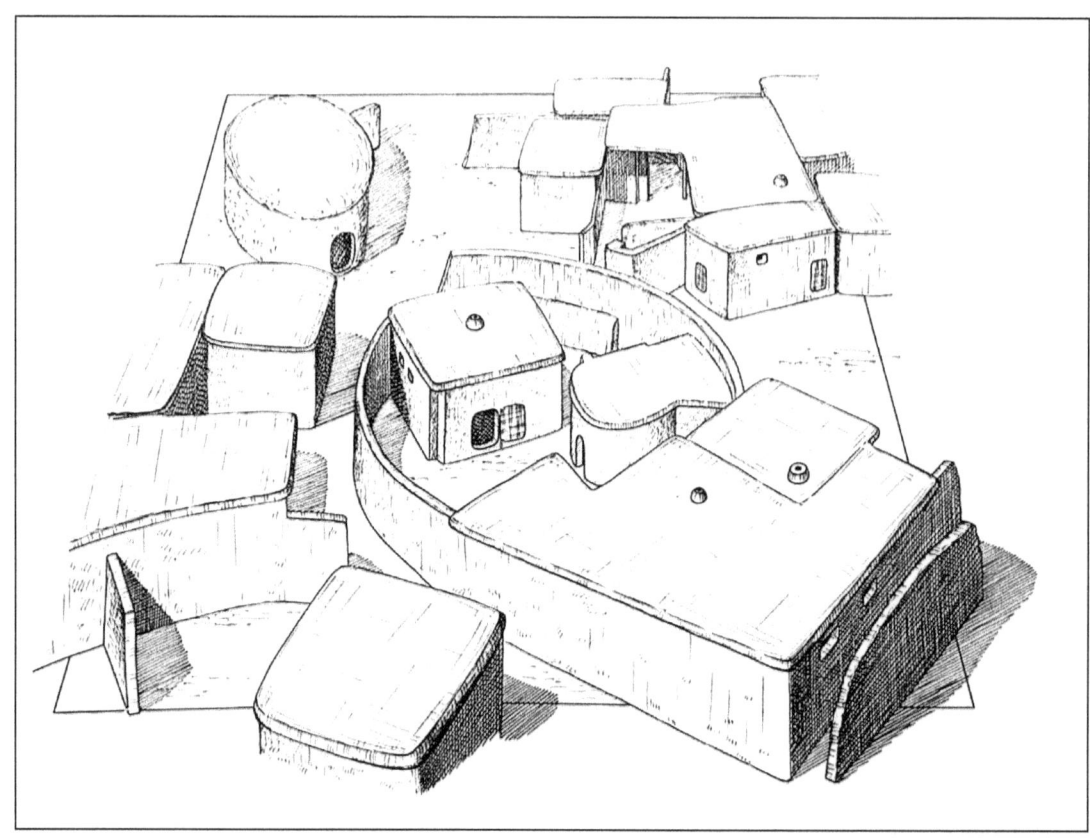

Fig. 31. Alikemektepesi. Reconstruction of settlement at level 310-210 cm

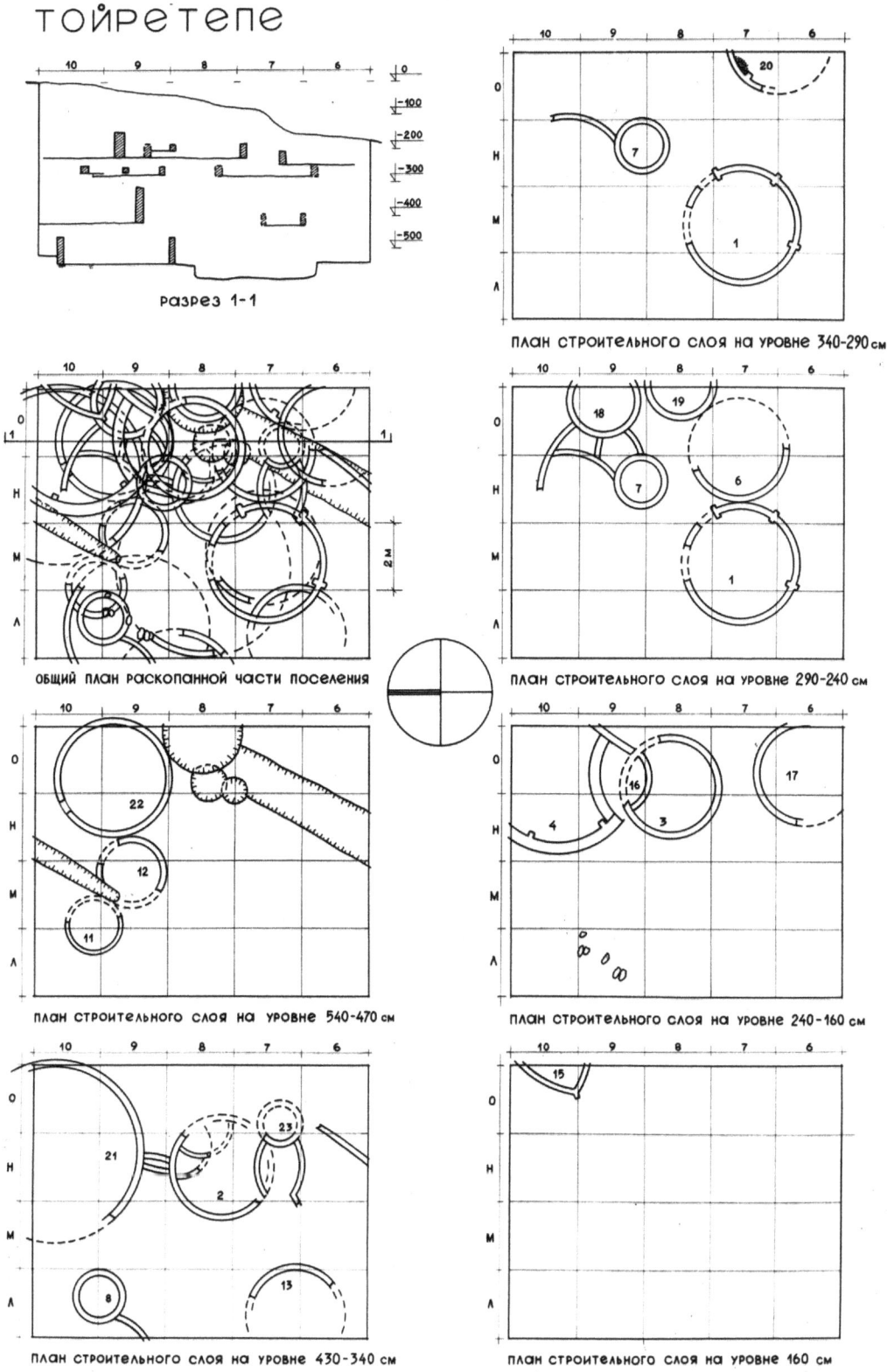

Fig. 32. Toyretepe. Plans and cut 1-1

Fig. 33. Toyretepe. Reconstruction of level 430-340 cm

Fig. 34. Toyretepe. Reconstruction of level 290-240 cm

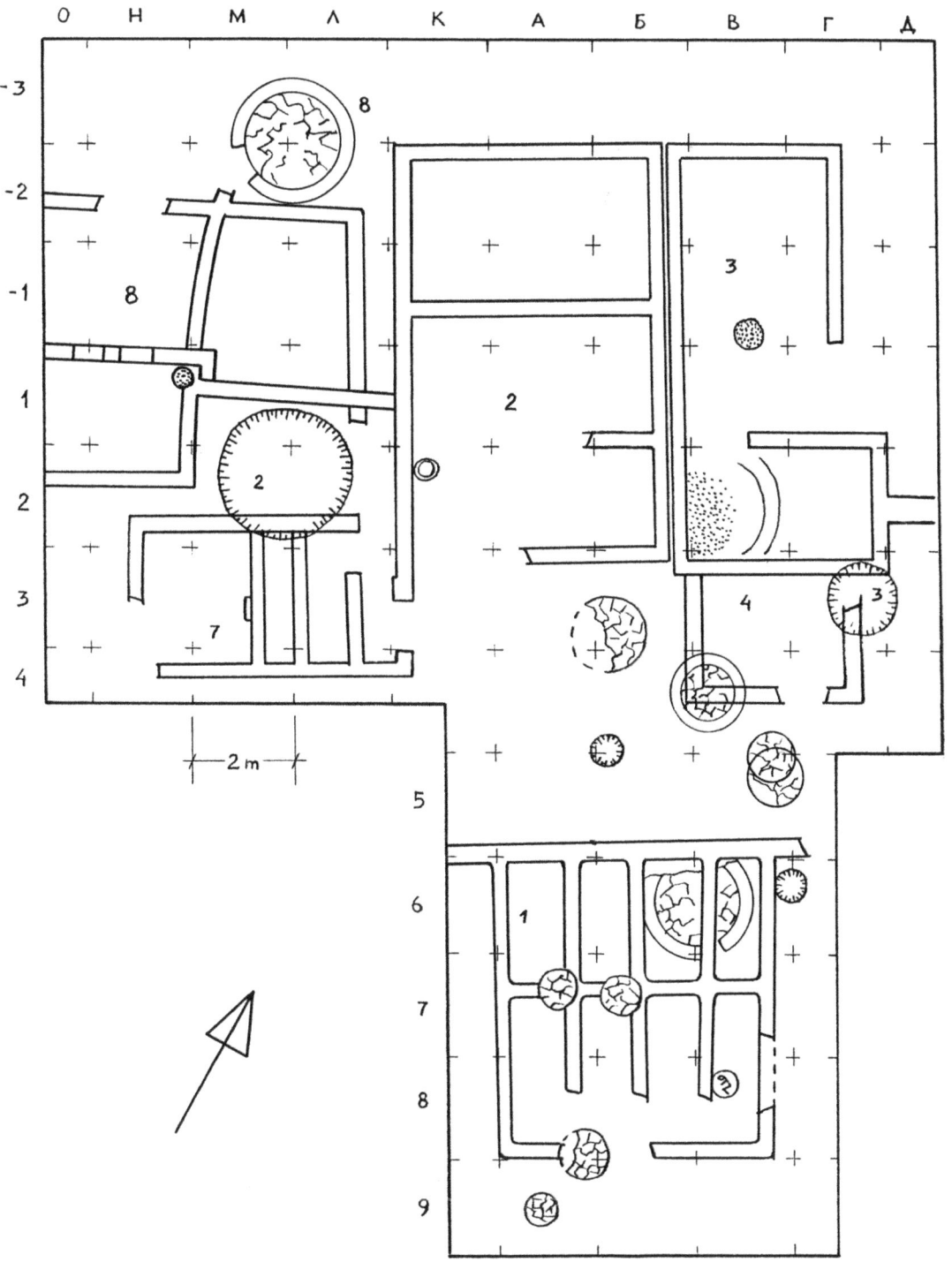

Fig. 35. Leylatepesi. Plan of excavation site

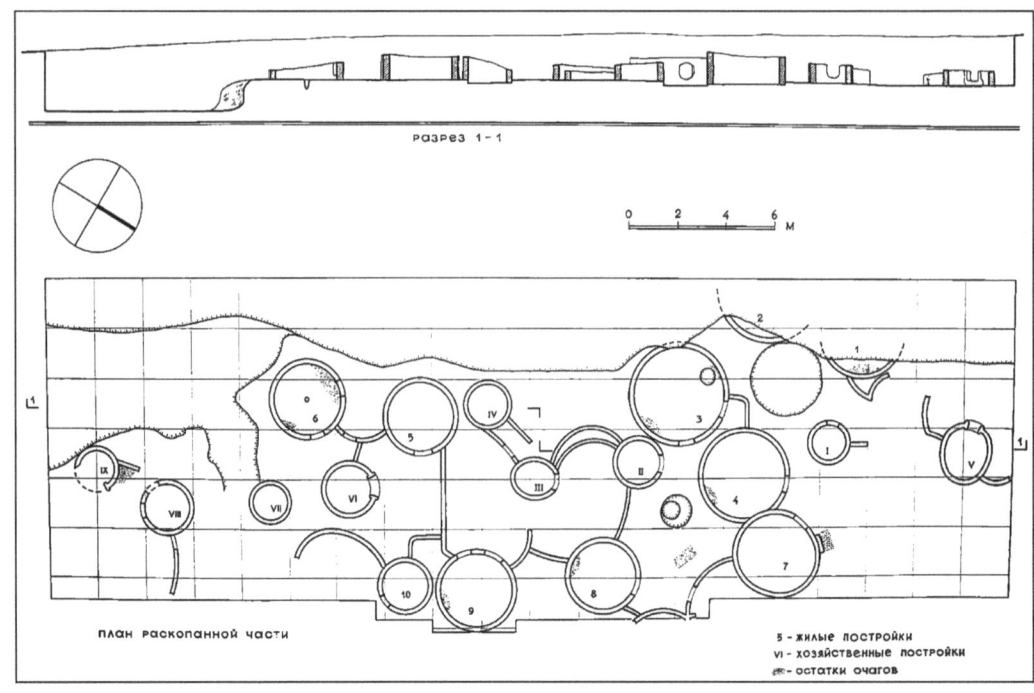

Fig. 36. Shomutepe. Plan and cut of excavation site

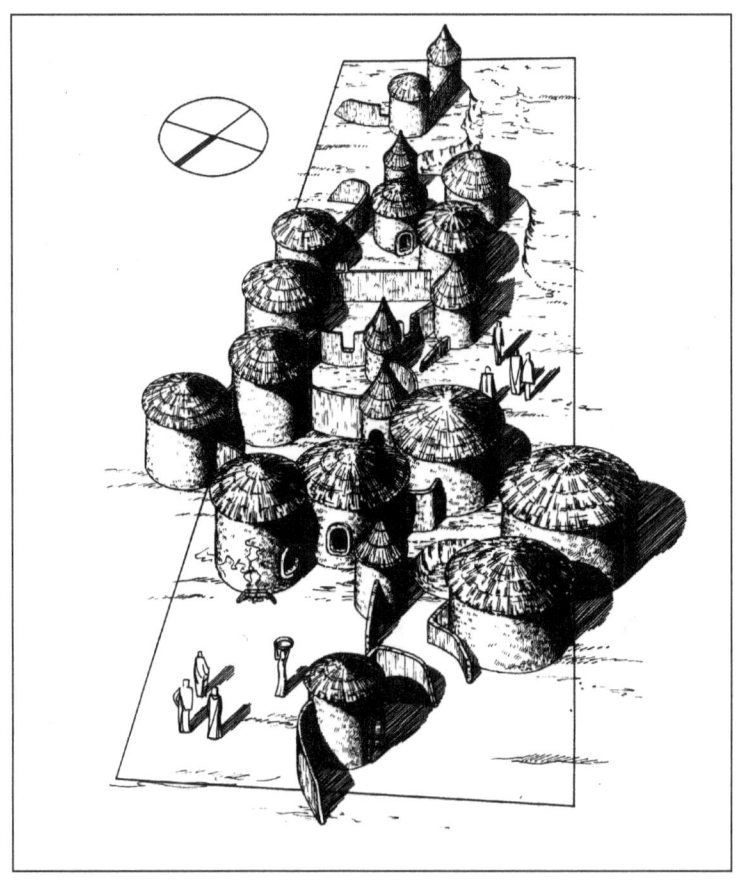

Fig. 37. Shomutepe. Reconstruction

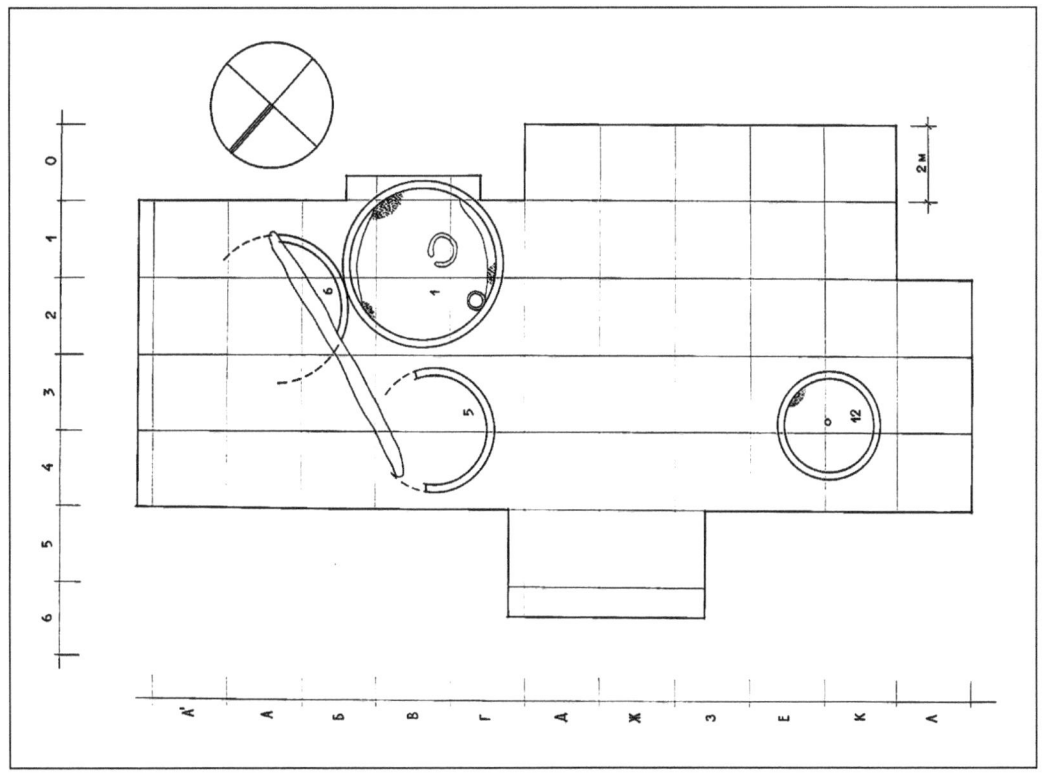

Fig. 38. Gargalartepesi. Plan of level 410-340 cm

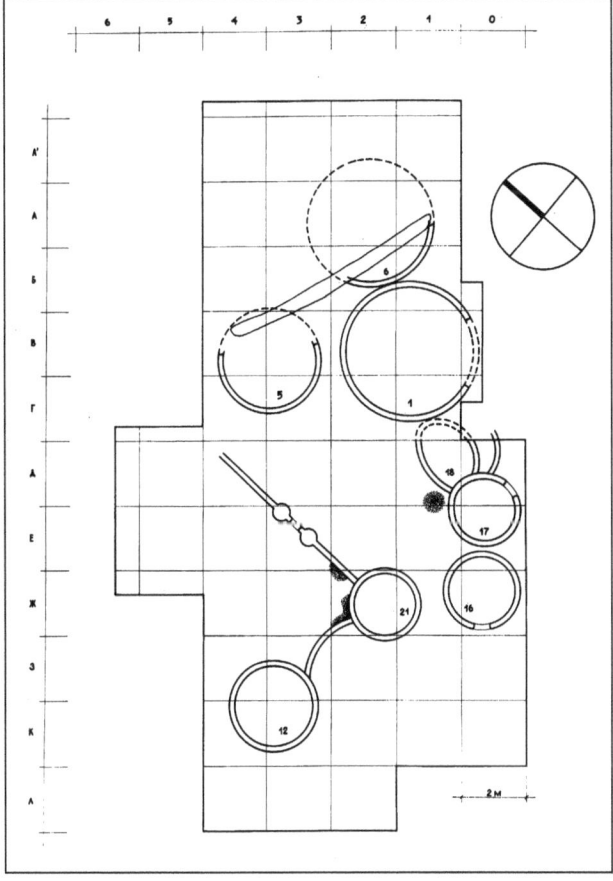

Fig. 39. Gargalartepesi. Plan of level 360-300 cm

Fig. 40. Gargalartepesi. Reconstruction of level 360-300 cm.

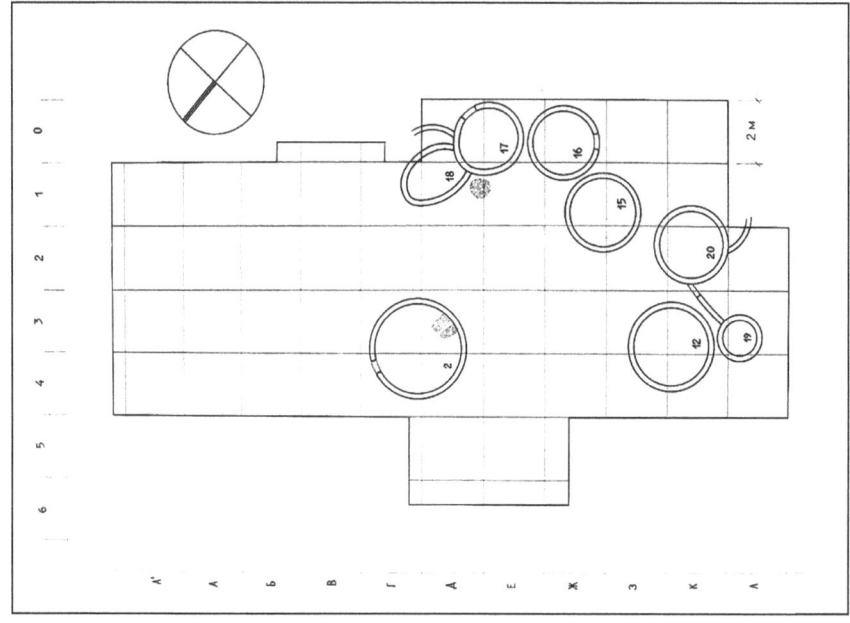

Fig. 41. Gargalartepesi. Plan of level 300-270 cm

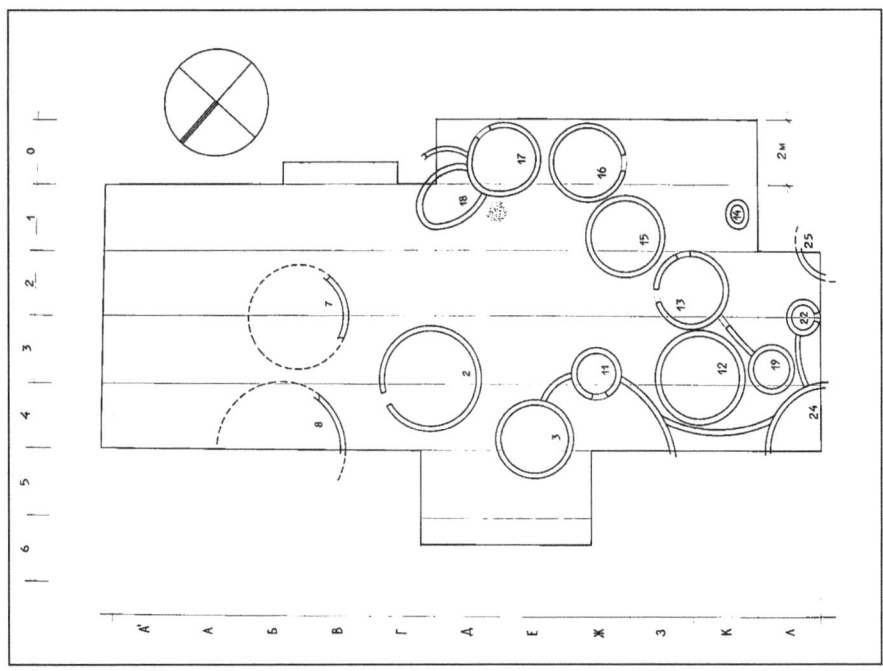

Fig. 42. Gargalartepesi. Plan of level 270-245 cm

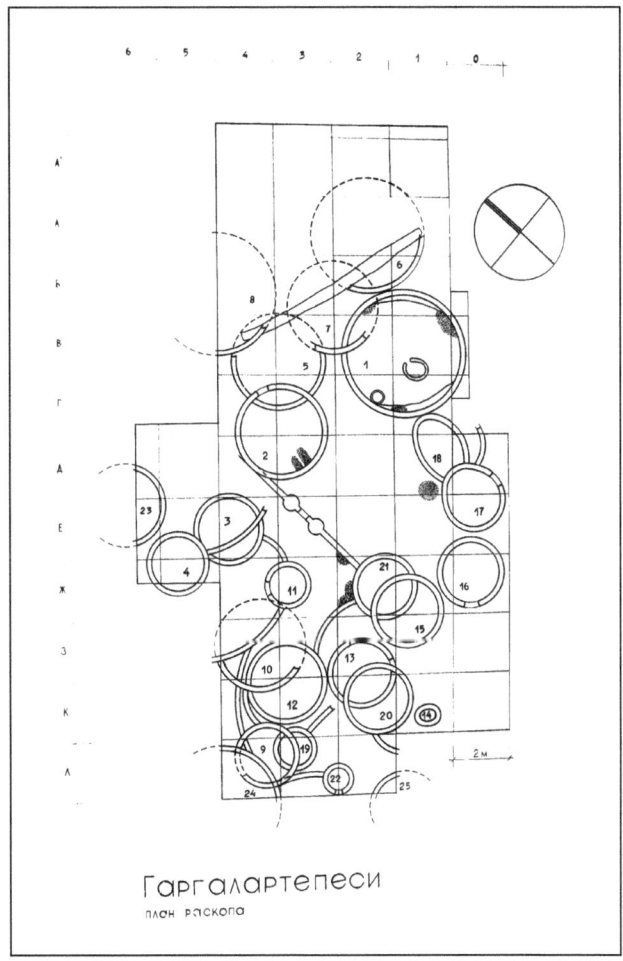

Fig. 43. Gargalartepesi. Consolidated plan of all layers

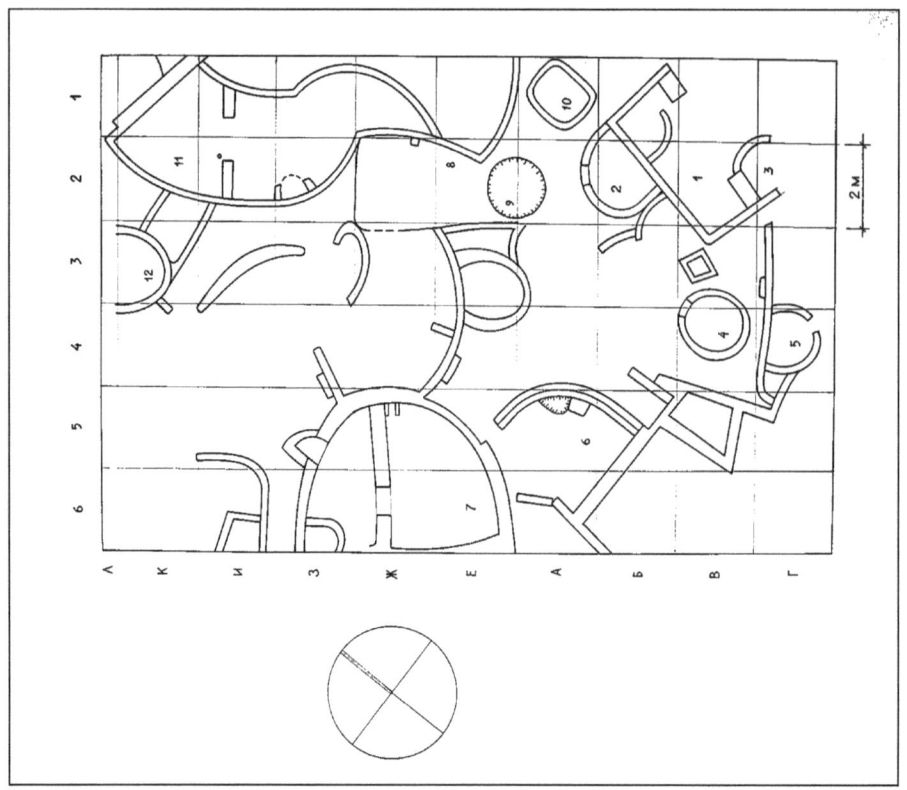

Fig. 44. Ilanlitepe. Plan of excavation site

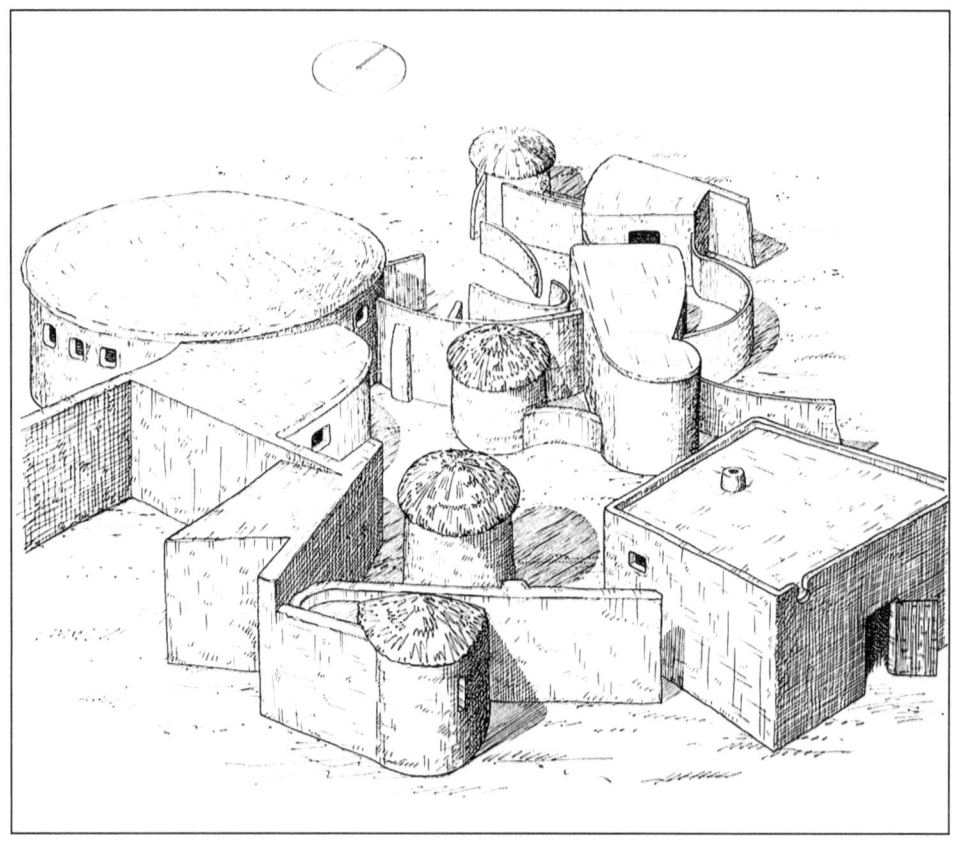

Fig. 45. Ilanlitepe. Reconstruction

*Fig. 46. Kultepe 1. Plan, cut and reconstruction.
Early Bronze Age V layer. Level 11.35 m*

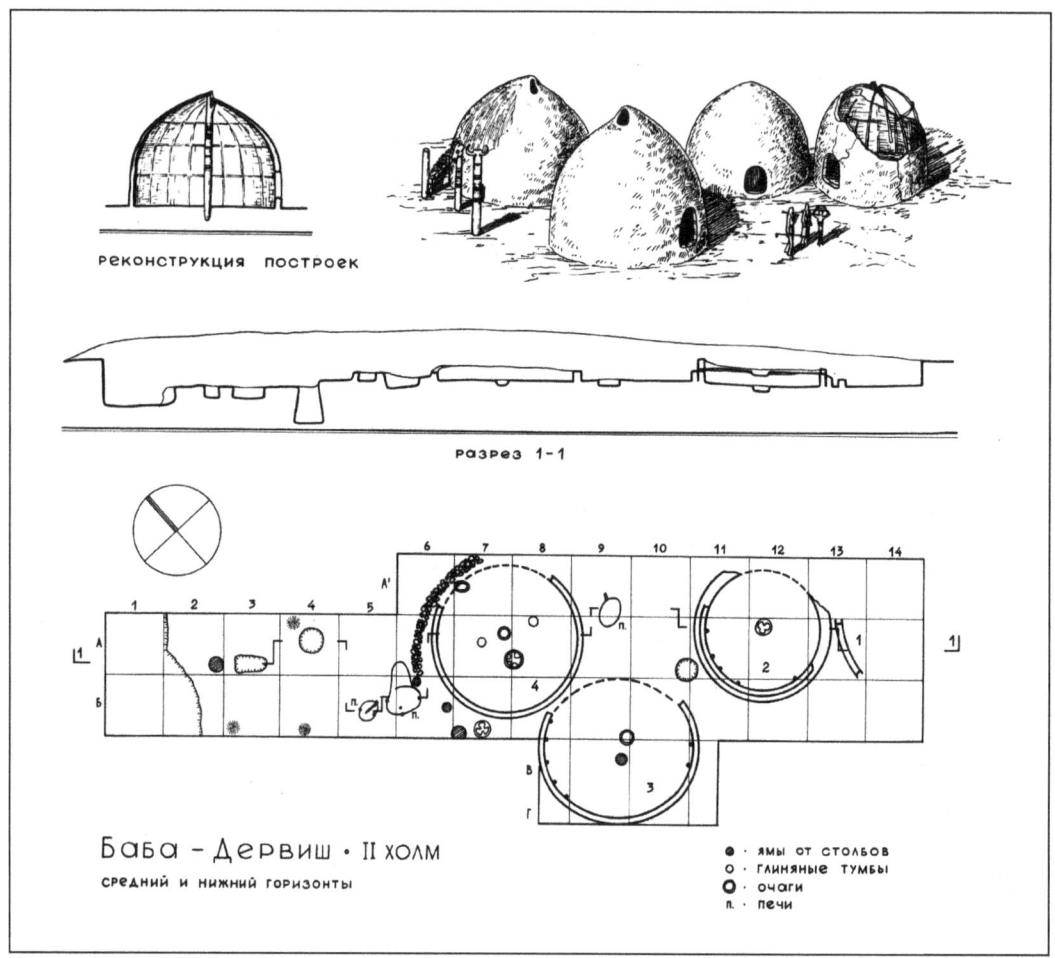

Fig. 47. Baba-Dervish. Hill II. Plan, cut and reconstruction.

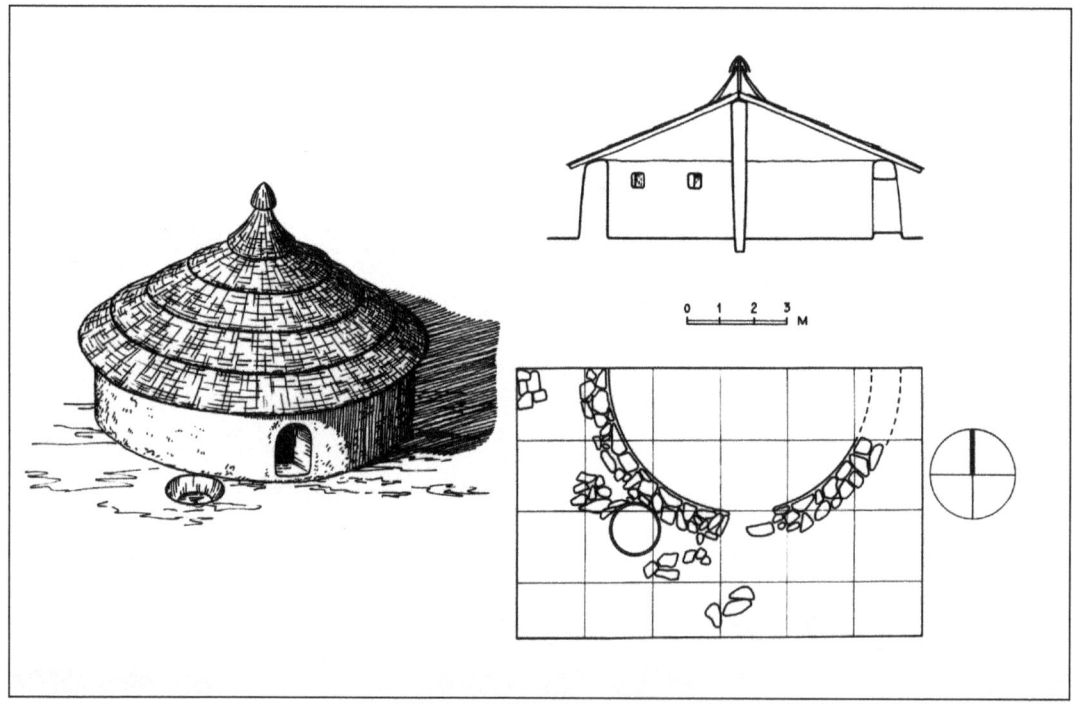

Fig. 48. Guneshtepe. Plan, cut and reconstruction of Early Bronze Age layer.

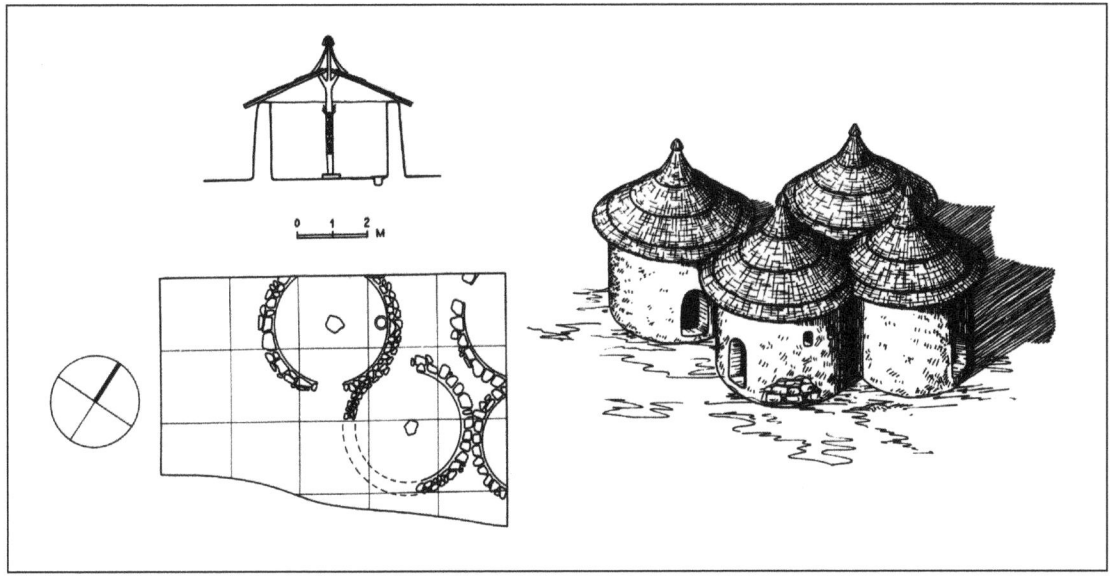

Fig. 49. Garakepektepe. Early Bronze Age layer. Plan, cut and reconstruction.

www.ingramcontent.com/pod-product-compliance
Lightning Source LLC
Chambersburg PA
CBHW061549010526
44115CB00023B/2985